Copyright © 2014 Authored By Cindy M. & Kenneth L. Quigley

All rights reserved.

ISBN: 1500527750
ISBN 13: 9781500527754

Dedicated to all our Super Mutts
and the people who love them.

Puppy Montessori

How to Raise a Puppy

A comprehensive puppy training system

Cindy M. Quigley

Kenneth L. Quigley

TABLE OF CONTENTS

Introduction

Chapter 1: Which Puppy Is Right for You?   1

Chapter 2: Developmental Levels   11

Chapter 3: Communication and Name Recognition   21

Chapter 4: The Nursery   27

Chapter 5: Potty Training   33

Chapter 6: Socialization   43

Chapter 7: Leash Walking   59

Chapter 8: Obedience   65

Chapter 9: Unwanted Behaviors   91

Chapter 10: Health and Vaccinations   111

Chapter 11: Grooming   131

Chapter 12: Nutrition   139

Chapter 13: Games to End Resource Guarding   151

Chapter 14: Toys and Chews   157

Chapter 15: Big Dog   167

Appendix A—Works Consulted   174

Appendix B—Dog Food Ratings and Glossary   176

Introduction

Happiness is a warm puppy. ~ Charles Schultz

Have you ever wondered how professional dog trainers have such well-behaved puppies or dogs? Many people say, "Of course, professional dog trainers know what to do." That is true to an extent. The real reason is that professional dog trainers DO what they know. Having knowledge and following through with that knowledge are two different things. With the Puppy Montessori program, we are giving you a summary of the best tools that we, as professional dog trainers, use to train puppies. The rest is up to you. You now have in your hands the knowledge, but do you have the willingness to do it? The bottom line is, you can waste your time doing the wrong things, or you can do what works. The Puppy Montessori program is a proven puppy training system that works.

The reason for writing this book is threefold. First, as pet care professionals we see how many dogs end up in shelters across the country. Since many of these dogs have behavioral problems, we know that if they had been raised properly in their initial home, they would not be there. People often surrender dogs between six and nine months of age. Therefore, our number one goal in writing this book is to help keep dogs in their homes and out of shelters. Second, as dog trainers, we have seen dogs with behavioral problems that the owner causes unknowingly. The fact that people are human—and try to raise dogs as such—just does not work. Third, many of our clients could have avoided frustration and mistakes if only they had had a source for answers in the beginning.

Our commitment to this book is for the dog. "The dog," an animal that we have brought into our world, has learned our language, can manipulate us in many ways, loves us unconditionally, and who by many people, is misunderstood. We also know that in helping the dog, we have to help the owner first. Humans cause most, if not all, behavioral problems in dogs; by helping one, you automatically help the other. People become more educated and dogs become more understood, creating a better dog/human bond, a lasting bond. In writing this book, we want people to realize that adopting a puppy is a very important step they need to take very seriously.

Dogs are not disposable or inanimate. They are living, breathing creatures that depend on us to take care of them. They did not ask us to take them into our world. As a society, we owe it to dogs to do everything possible to understand them as what they are so we can provide them with everything necessary to grow and flourish as "dogs." We need to remember that we are the ones with higher intelligence; with that comes great responsibility. It is our duty as caretakers. There are no excuses.

Congratulations on taking the first and most important step in your new puppy's life, educating yourself on puppy. For most people, getting a puppy is a very exciting time and can be an extremely frustrating time. The excitement comes from having this little furry playful ball of cuteness in our presence. The frustration comes from not understanding what this ball of cuteness needs, really needs.

We have heard many complaints and frustrations from puppy owners regarding things such as potty training and destructive behaviors. In fact, all of these behaviors are not "bad" behaviors to the puppy but rather just a puppy "being" a puppy. The puppy Montessori program will give you all the tools to mitigate these so-called undesired behaviors and therefore establish "desired" behaviors with your puppy. This alone will help ease the majority of your frustration when it comes to raising a puppy.

We want to begin by saying that there is no EASY way to raise a puppy, and those who tell you they have an easy way to raise a puppy are lying. Raising a puppy takes time—lots of YOUR time and commitment. The puppy Montessori program will help make the puppy-raising process easier and less frustrating than if you do not use the program, but it will still take time and commitment on your part.

Just as you need to prepare your home and family for a new baby, you also need to prepare your home and family for a new "baby" dog. The Puppy Montessori program teaches you how to do just that. The puppy Montessori program will give you the tools and knowledge needed to make the puppy experience an enjoyable one for both you and your new puppy. This program will enable you to set a foundation to grow your puppy into a well-adjusted, well-mannered, stable adult dog.

The Puppy Montessori program is a resource that you can go to when you have questions about leadership, feeding, potty training, socialization, vaccinations, toys, treats, obedience, destructive behaviors, leash walking, and much more. By purchasing this book, you have taken the first and most important step in building a relationship with your new best friend. By reading and utilizing the techniques described in this book, you will be able to enjoy your puppy and realize that it does not have to be such a tiresome, frustrating experience.

We do not know of any new expecting parents that do not have questions about parenthood. They buy books, search online, and ask friends and relatives to help, oftentimes months before the delivery. Many people have their parents or grandparents stay with them the first few weeks of their new bundle of joy's life just to help with the adjustment of having a helpless, vulnerable being in their presence. They learn everything about feeding, potty training, immunizations, illnesses, growth and development, socialization, education, and bonding. They prepare a nursery and buy clothing, furniture, toys, bottles, etc. We all know that human babies do not know all the rules of the modern family. After all, they are helpless creatures and just need the basics of food, water, shelter, and love. We teach them the rules of the family as they grow. Human babies do not come with a spoken language, so we also have to teach them ours. We want you to take, you NEED to take the same responsibility with your new "baby dog"—and, yes, it is a "baby," and it will require many of the same preparations as bringing home a human baby. Stop seeing it as a puppy and start seeing it as a "baby dog." You are bringing a baby into your home, not a human baby, but a baby nonetheless that has a set of needs all its own. Its needs are similar but different from a human baby, but it is your responsibility to know what those needs are, just as you would if bringing a human baby into your home.

It is ridiculous to assume you can bring a baby home and leave it to its own devices. You would not do it with a human baby, and you should not do it with a dog baby. It is a baby. Let us say it again: IT IS A BABY. So many people bring a puppy home on Friday and leave that same eight-week-old or so being at home, alone, on Monday. They assume it will act like an adult, sit quietly, and wait for them to come home. Again, this is a being that has only been alive for eight weeks. Would you leave an eight-week-old human baby alone all day to its own devices and expect it to fend for itself? No. Dogs are perpetual two-year-old self-serving opportunists. We would not leave a two-year-old human baby at home alone and expect it to be alive when we returned. Why then do we expect another species (puppy) to not only be alive when we leave it alone but also expect it to be an adult, know what is expected from it, and not explore everything left to its devices? Do dogs desert their young at eight weeks old? No. Puppies stay in a dog pack and learn from the pack until they are mature enough and strong enough to move on and start their own pack or join a new one to reproduce. The fact that we take puppies from their pack at eight weeks of age does not make them adults and is not natural in the dog world. They are babies when we adopt them, and we need to provide for them. There is no fast track to this process. If you adopt a puppy (baby dog), you have to put in your time. Please, if you are not ready for this responsibility, as it is a great one, then do not adopt a puppy. Maybe an adult dog is a better fit for you. Either way, do not assume that the new dog you adopt knows what humans expect of it. The only way dogs know what we expect is to teach them. If you are not willing to be a teacher, a dog is not for you.

Just as human babies have levels of development that have milestones, so do dog babies. The Puppy Montessori program identifies those developmental levels and the appropriate things to teach during these different levels of development. Since we are not dogs, we need to be the best surrogate dog mom or dog dad that we can be. The Puppy Montessori program will help you do just that. Congratulations on your new puppy and let the training begin…

How to use this book

Puppy Montessori is a proven puppy training system. The system will provide the best result ONLY if you implement the complete system. Do not use only part of the system. Read this book in its entirety before implementation. Each chapter of this book has elements that you will implement daily with your new puppy. For instance, you will set up a nursery, work on socialization, potty training, leash walking, and obedience, all during the same time on a daily basis. You will find information on each of these topics in different chapters. In the later chapters, you will find information on toys and nutrition, which you will need when you first bring your puppy home. We strongly recommend you read the book before you bring a new puppy into your home. However, if you already have a puppy in the house, do not skip chapters. Start from the beginning, and do not worry if you have done something wrong.

Throughout the book, you will see sections called "notes" and "alerts." Notes are about things we feel are important and noteworthy for you to remember. Alerts are about things that are extremely important to either implement or avoid.

You will find that the term "he" is used to identify the puppy. We use this only for the ease of writing; it is not meant to discriminate toward either sex.

Chapter 1

Which Puppy Is Right for You?

Until one has loved an animal, a part of one's soul remains unawakened. ~ Anatole France

Congratulations on your new puppy! Your new "baby" dog. Regardless of how you obtained your puppy—from a shelter or rescue group, a pet store, a breeder, a box outside a store that said "free puppies," or from an ad in the paper—all puppies have the same basic requirements and have the same developmental levels throughout their lifetime. Keep in mind, however, that all puppies and different breeds have their own personalities, drives, and energy levels.

For instance, some breeds have high-energy levels, such as the terriers — Jack Russell, Wheaton terrier, Cairn terrier, etc. These dogs have high exercise requirements.

Some breeds are known for their intelligence and high-energy levels; if left to their own devices, they can wreak havoc on a home. This includes breeds in the herding group such as the Australian shepherd, Border collie, Australian cattle dog (heelers), and the Shetland sheepdog.

The working breeds, such as the Boxer, Rottweiler, Doberman, and German shepherd, can become aggressive and unstable in a home that does not understand them and meet their needs as "working dogs."

Toy breeds, although small and cute, are known for being barkers and difficult to house train. The bully breeds, such as the English bulldog, are known to have low exercise requirements, but they have a reputation as being headstrong and bullheaded.

The curly coated and longhaired breeds, such as the poodle, Bichon frise, Shih-Tzu, Cocker spaniel, or any mixture of these breeds, have increased grooming requirements that will take time and money on your part.

Of course, mixed breeds known for their hybrid vigor or hardiness are a combination of many breeds and can have characteristics of any of the breeds from which they descend. Although this is not a full rundown on all the different breeds and their characteristics, you get the idea. Do the research.

So, as you can see, the first thing you should do when preparing for a new puppy is to decide what breed and energy level will fit your lifestyle. Ultimately, before you bring a puppy home, you should research what breeds you are interested in and their character traits. You may even find that a puppy is not what you need at all; an older dog may better fit your situation. You may decide to adopt from a shelter or rescue group or purchase a puppy from a reputable breeder. Whatever you decide, bringing a puppy home is a big responsibility that requires a lot of time and effort for the first six months to one year. If you work full time, do not have the resources to send the puppy to day care, or do not have a relative to help, then a puppy is not for you. It is not reasonable to think you can bring a puppy home and leave it alone for eight to ten hours. This will cause major behavioral problems, and it is likely your puppy will end up one of the many being "rehomed" or surrendered to a shelter. If you purchased this book and this one paragraph made you realize that a puppy is not for you, then we have met our number one goal in keeping dogs out of shelters and we are happy with that. However, if you are one that has the time, resources, and family support to bring a puppy home, then your journey is just beginning, and we believe you have taken the first step in doing it right.

If you, like many others, did not research which breed is right for you, and you just happened upon a puppy or made an impulse decision, and now you have a puppy, this book is especially for you. If you are a first-time puppy owner, then this book is definitely for you.

As you will see in this book, where you get your puppy is also important. The developmental stages of a puppy's life begin at birth. How your puppy is handled and socialized during these crucial stages is very important to its growth and development throughout its life. For instance, a puppy that is restricted from all human contact during these crucial weeks can develop temperament issues and become almost feral or wild. This type of puppy is the most difficult puppy to raise, as it is like raising a wild dog in your home. They do not bond to humans like their well-socialized counterparts, and they are fearful, timid, and often aggressive and unpredictable. They are never truly comfortable around humans and do not make good pets, especially for inexperienced or first-time dog owners. These puppies require a lot of proper socialization and oftentimes need an experienced "rehabilitator" to step in and help.

We cannot say there is any "right" way to obtain a puppy. Each way to acquiring a puppy has its pros and cons. Arguments ensue about the puppy-adopting experience. Many people think adopting from a breeder is the way to go because "you know what you are getting." We will agree that if you purchase your puppy from a professional (reputable) breeder, that this statement can be true. Professional breeders have a long history of breeding one breed of dog. They have lineage that goes back years, often decades. They have bred out as many negative traits as possible of that particular breed, such as common health problems and temperament issues. Their entire goal is to make the breed better. They do it for the love of the breed; not the money. You can see the parents, will be given the lineage of grandparents and great-grandparents, and the puppy will be health certified. Its sire and dam will have been tested for negative traits of the individual breed, such as hip dysplasia in large breeds. The breeder will have worked toward breeding out such things as deafness in Dalmatians, allergies, heart problems, temperament problems, etc. If you purchase from a breeder you should research the common health and temperament problems of that breed and question the breeder about them.

There are reasons that you may not "know what you are getting" when it comes to purchasing from a breeder. Many people coin themselves as "breeders." Many of them can be categorized as amateur breeders, also known as "backyard breeders." Being in the pet care industry, we have seen many well-meaning people who have two dogs of the same breed and decide to breed them, not knowing the health or temperament history of either dog's lineage. Some were very good at taking care of and socializing the litter and turned out some great puppies. We have also seen people breed siblings to each other, ending up with small unhealthy litters and puppies born with cleft palate. Many so-called breeders that engage in "line breeding" put out puppies that have major behavioral and temperament issues along with many health issues. Of course, we have also seen puppies that were "sold" as purebreds at a so-called reasonable price, and as they grow, it is clear they are mixed breeds. Some of these amateur breeders see it as a quick way to make money.

Therefore, if you decide to purchase from a breeder—amateur or professional—do your research. Ask many questions, such as how the breeder purchased the breeding pair, how many litters do they allow each bitch to have, (a reputable breeder will have fewer litters per bitch, a breeder trying to make money will have many.) How long have they bred dogs, etc. Look at the facilities where the puppies are housed. Is it clean? Are the puppies clean? Do people handle the puppies regularly? Are the parents healthy and of good temperament? If you have children, ask if the puppies have been exposed to children. How does the breeder socialize the puppies?

When you do your research, you will find that a professional breeder that satisfies all the pros in the aforementioned text will often come with a premium price tag. This is why many amateur breeders continue to be in demand. Many people want that cute purebred or designer puppy at a low price. Caveat emptor: "buyer beware."

Many people recommend adopting from a shelter or animal control facility, and we agree that if you can give a home to a puppy or dog that is surely going to be euthanized, then that is a win. Especially since, according to the ASPCA, "approximately five million to seven million companion animals enter animal shelters nationwide every year, and approximately three million to four million are euthanized (60 percent of dogs and 70 percent of cats). Shelter intakes are about evenly divided between those animals relinquished by owners and those picked up by animal control. These are national estimates; the percentage of euthanasia may vary from state to state."

When adopting from animal control or a kill shelter, you do not necessarily know "what you are going to get," as when buying from a professional breeder, but sometimes you do. The ASPCA states that twenty-five percent of dogs that enter local shelters are purebred. Therefore, it is possible to find a purebred puppy in a shelter. Just know when adopting from a kill shelter or animal control that many of these puppies or dogs are there for only a short time and nothing is known about their past. Some of these dogs come with illnesses such as kennel cough, worms, etc., so it is necessary to take your puppy to the vet straight from one of these facilities. When you adopt from a kill shelter ask to spend time with the puppy and ask for as much information as possible that the staff can give you. Pay close attention to the card on the kennel; if they are known, take heed of behavioral issues such as aggression, fear, etc. If you are not an experienced dog owner, you will want to adopt the puppy or dog with the fewest number of issues. It makes no sense to adopt a puppy with behavioral problems if you can adopt a healthy, stable adult dog from the same shelter. Also, note that animal control and shelters do not always have puppies, so you may have to make several trips to find what you are looking for. There are many wonderful dogs in kill shelters, and it is worth it to make this an option on your quest to finding a new puppy. Many people think that there is something wrong with dogs in shelters when, in fact, that is not true. Some may have behavioral problems that the inexperienced dog owner is not prepared for, but we will cover that in a later book. Many great dogs end up in shelters because of a death in the family, a move, or just an irresponsible owner. To make the adoption process easier when going to a shelter, it is advisable to take a dog trainer with you to help pick the right dog for your situation.

Rescue groups and no-kill shelters are great ways to find a puppy. These facilities often get their dogs from kill shelters if they seem suitable for adoption. The pros to this form of adoption are that many of the animals in their care have been there long enough to enable the staff to develop information on the temperament of the animal. Most rescue groups do not have a facility but foster out their dogs to individuals until the dogs can be adopted. Most dogs have been spayed, neutered, and brought up to good health. They have also been vaccinated with the proper vaccines for the age of the dog. With puppies, some of them are born at the shelter, so they can tell you the temperament of at least the mother. Puppies born in no-kill shelters and to rescue groups generally have been handled and socialized enough to negate any temperament issues. The cons are that some no-kill shelters and rescue groups rescue "every" dog possible, disregarding temperament issues or long-term health issues. Therefore, if the staff tells you that the puppy or dog has any issues such as separation anxiety, aggression, fearfulness, etc., then you may want to choose one without such issues to ease your frustration once you get your puppy home.

The pet store is another way some people acquire puppies. Now we are not talking about the large box pet stores, they do not "sell" puppies but rather let rescue groups use their facilities to adopt out dogs. We are talking about the pet stores in the malls and stand-alone small pet stores that "sell" dogs and puppies. These types of stores sell so-called purebred or designer puppies at a very high price. The problem with getting a puppy at these types of pet stores is that you definitely will not "know what you are getting." We have seen puppies come from pet stores sold at top dollar and advertised as pure breeds that are clearly mixed breed puppies. Many of these stores get their puppies for bottom dollar through puppy mills. We could go on and on about puppy mills, but for the sake of keeping this section short, just know that puppy mills keep dogs in deplorable conditions and breed the females repeatedly. They do not socialize the animals or do anything for the welfare of their dogs or puppies. The dogs are kept in tiny wire cages twenty-four hours a day, seven days a week, three hundred sixty-five days a year, and always in filthy conditions. The females are used only for breeding. Many puppies coming from puppy mills are difficult to potty train, as they have never been out of a kennel and have always eliminated in the kennel. If the pet store has a sign that says, "We don't buy from puppy mills," then ask them where they get their puppies. Some of them get them from "middle men" who obtained them from puppy mills. Many of them get them from backyard breeders and cannot tell you anything regarding the lineage, temperament, or health of the puppy. We have seen several "pet store" puppies with major health and temperament issues and puppies that are clearly not the breed sold to the buyer. One thing you can know for sure is that professional breeders never sell their puppies to pet stores, period. We do not recommend purchasing a puppy from a pet store that "sells" puppies.

Of course, there are many other ways to obtain a puppy. There is always the sign or newspaper ad that says, "Free puppies"; there is someone outside a store with a box of them that says, "Free puppies," and countless other ways. The great thing about adopting a puppy is just that, it is a "puppy." Therefore, no matter where you choose to get your puppy from, they are very resilient and generally come with few innate behavioral problems. It depends on how much of a gambler you are as to where you adopt your puppy. It is always advisable to do it methodically rather than impulsively, but no matter how you decide to bring a new "baby dog" into your home, just know you are taking on a lifelong commitment.

There is no such thing as a "free" puppy. It is not reasonable to think you can bring a puppy home and have no expenses associated with it. Even though you do not pay any money to acquire the puppy, right away you have an expense for food, bowl, toys, leash, collar, vaccinations, etc. Following is a table from the ASPCA of the average minimum yearly cost of owning a dog. The ASPCA also states, "This chart represents the estimated minimum cost of humane care. You shouldn't expect to pay less than this, and you should definitely be prepared to pay more. Don't forget to factor in the costs of unexpected veterinary care, as well as boarding facilities, pet sitters and dog walkers, if you plan to use them."

Costs	Sm Dog	Med. Dog	Lg. Dog
Food	$55	$120	$235
Recurring medical	$210	$235	$260
Toys/treats	$40	$55	$75
License	$15	$15	$15
Health Insurance	$225	$225	$225
Misc.	$35	$45	$65
Spay/neuter	$190	$200	$220
Other initial medical	$70	$70	$70
Collar/leash	$25	$30	$35
Carrier	$40	$60	
Crate	$35	$95	$125
Training class	$110	$110	$110
Grooming	$264	$320	$408
First year total costs	$1,314	$1,580	$1,843

Keep in mind this is just an estimate. Prices will vary based on the health of your pet, temperament, grooming requirements, and the area of the country you live in. This is just to give you an idea of the commitment you will be taking on when you decide to bring a puppy home. Of course, this is only the monetary part; there is also a large commitment of time on your part and on the part of your family.

This table also does not take into consideration the cost of new carpet, if you allow your puppy to eliminate on it, or new couches, tables, pillows, shoes, chairs, etc., if you allow the puppy to chew on them. Notice we say, "**If you allow.**" You can eliminate these costs with the puppy Montessori program.

It is also important to get your whole family's input on what type of dog they want, or if they want one at all. You may find that everyone in the family has different ideas on the type of puppy they want. People turn in many puppies to shelters because one family member brought a puppy home without consulting the other members of the family. Discuss such things as size, breed, short hair, or long hair, etc. If everyone is on the same page as to the type of puppy they are interested in, it will make things much easier for the whole family.

Littermates

We need to take this time to discuss littermates. Breeders or rescue groups sometimes talk people into getting littermates so that "the puppy will have a playmate." Getting littermates is never a good idea for a few different reasons. 1) It is difficult to control two puppies. 2) Littermates will influence each other. If you have one puppy that has a higher energy level and drive, he will influence the other puppy and can make training very difficult. 3) You will have more time and expense associated with the puppy-raising process. When training multiple puppies, you need to work with them separately and preferably by two handlers (one for each puppy). 4) Littermates have been together since birth. They know each other better than they will ever learn about or care to know you. As long as they are together, they are more interested in each other than in the handler. Littermates are very difficult to train for most people, and we do not recommend adopting littermates.

As stated before, you should put as much thought into bringing a baby dog home as you would in bringing a baby human into your home. Consider everything to make the best possible choice for you, your family, and your new puppy.

Chapter 2

Developmental levels

There is no psychiatrist in the world like a puppy licking your face.
~Ben Williams

Just as human babies go through different developmental levels during certain intervals, so do canine babies. All dog owners should know what these developmental levels are and what level their puppy is at. Knowing these developmental levels will not only help you understand why your puppy is behaving in certain ways, but it also will help you eliminate potential situations that can cause behavioral problems in your pet. Many people who bring a puppy into their home unknowingly cause behavioral problems, because they do not understand these critical periods in their puppy's life. Psychologists use the term "critical period" to describe a specific time in a dog's life when certain experiences have a lasting effect on their psychological development.

If you do a web search on "developmental levels of dogs," you will find information from several different resources. Each of them has some different terminology and age ranges for each level, but for the most part, each explains the same levels of development. It is important to know that it is not cut in stone that each stage of development will start at X week and end at X week. Each level may be a little shorter or longer, depending on the puppy. We have narrowed it down for you and will give you information on the things you should do or not do with your puppy during these critical periods.

Developmental levels of dogs start when they are born. For the purposes of this book, we will focus on the stages that are the most important to the reader, from seven weeks to one year. However, please note that the way your pup was "raised" and handled from birth to seven weeks plays a large part in the pup's personality and temperament. A good example of this is a puppy that belonged to a client of ours.

Case Study:

A client of ours was working at an animal control facility. At the time, a litter of puppies was surrendered. She adopted one of these puppies because it reminded her of a dog she had owned that had passed away. The only information provided was that the litter was born under a trailer, with no human contact whatsoever. She was an animal lover obviously; she worked at animal control and had previously owned a dog rescue. She brought the puppy home at eleven weeks old. Now, what she did next is very important. The puppy already had bad imprinting during the early stages of its life with no human contact. It was very fearful and hid behind the toilet for the next three to four weeks. This is not normal for an eleven-week-old puppy. During this time, the well-meaning person would take it food, talk lovingly to it, pet it, and tell him "it was OK." All the while, she allowed it to stay hidden in the bathroom behind the toilet. Eventually she coaxed the puppy out. She did what she could to take him out on walks but still kept him socially isolated because of his "fear" of people. He eventually started to become aggressive with people and with other pets. He would come to us for grooming services once a month. He never became used to the process, would always shake, would often defecate with copious amounts of diarrhea, and would sometimes offer to bite. We eventually told her we could not take him for grooming any longer. He became comfortable with the owner and her family, but he always lived in fear should anything out of the ordinary happen. It was a dog she had to "manage," and she chose to do so. The sad thing is that we are sure there were many other "good" dogs of good temperament that were euthanized that she could have chosen over this one.

We know the puppy was isolated during some of the critical periods; this alone can cause a dog to have temperament issues. The fact that they allowed him to stay isolated during the remaining four weeks of a critical period made the situation worse. Now, the damage could have already been done, but had she known about the critical periods of a dog's life and what to do during them, she might have helped this dog become a better-socialized pet. What she did by coddling it while it remained in the bathroom was in fact reinforcing the fearfulness. Basically dooming the animal.

We hope this exhibits why it is so important to not only know where your puppy came from but also to know the developmental levels and what to do during them for the psychological health of your new puppy.

As stated before, the developmental stages of a dog's life are not cut and dried; puppies do not go through them at exactly the same time. Each developmental stage can vary by days or even weeks and from puppy to puppy. The basic developmental stages are as follows:

Newborn: birth to seven weeks

This is a period of rapid growth and development. When puppies are born, they are born with their ears and eyes closed and have no teeth. This is a period when puppies rely on the mother to provide everything. Over the next seven weeks, they will learn to see, hear, balance, walk, bark, and play. They will also learn to eat solid food. The most critical element of behavior during this period is that they learn how to live in a pack structure. Through play, they will learn to recognize the higher-ranking siblings and the lower-ranking pack members. From the mother and siblings they will learn discipline and bite inhibition.

"Bite inhibition" is simply when the puppy refrains from a full bite while playing with others; he "inhibits" his full biting potential. They learn this from their mother when they are suckling and from other puppies when they are playing. If a puppy bites too hard while suckling, the mother will get up and walk away. If the puppy bites his mother too hard in play, she will growl and bite or "correct" him for this, ending the play session. If the puppy bites other siblings too hard, they will run away and stop playing; some may retaliate—either way, ending the play session. In this way, the puppy learns "when I bite hard, play ends, period." Since puppies like to suckle and play, they learn to inhibit the bite to continue doing the things they love to do. This generally occurs around five to seven weeks old, which is why it is not recommended to take a puppy from its litter until seven weeks of age or older.

During this time, puppies also need to be socialized with humans, or the pups may become feral or wild. They need to have positive experiences with men, women, and children. This is why it is important to know where your puppy came from. A good breeder should handle them daily and keep the nursery area clean. The breeder should start taking them outside once they can walk and should get them used to the normal sights and sounds of a home. The breeder should encourage different people to handle the puppies and expose them to as many new things as possible without stressing them. If you are getting your puppy from someone who does not care if you take the puppy before seven weeks of age, the person clearly does not understand puppy development. The person is obviously an amateur. You should leave and get a puppy elsewhere.

The next and most important stage to you, the new puppy owner, is the socialization stage.

Socialization or imprinting stage: -seven to sixteen weeks

Also called the toddler stage, this stage of development is considered to be THE most important developmental level of your dog's life. This developmental level sets the stage for what type of dog your new puppy will become. Puppies in this age group are growing daily, not only physically but also mentally and behaviorally. During this stage of development, it is imperative to socialize your puppy to as many different sights, sounds, people, and animals and to as many new situations as possible—but in the right way, which we will explain in detail in the chapter on socialization.

During this stage your puppy will be going through what is called a "fear-imprinting phase." The fear-imprinting phase simply means that whatever your puppy comes into contact with that causes fear or pain can stay with him for life. Your puppy also will be "imprinted" to everything positive in his life. Therefore, everything you expose your new puppy to should be kept positive.

For instance, let's say your puppy is following you around while you are doing housework. If you start vacuuming, then trip over the cord and knock something off a table, causing a loud noise that scares the puppy, he may run away and hide. That may imprint him to be afraid of the vacuum cleaner. If so, you will have to work on getting him used to the vacuum cleaner with positive methods. Now, just because puppies go through this "fear-imprinting" period does not mean you should keep them away from everything; in fact, that is the worst thing you can do.

The fear-imprint period is a developmental stage during which the puppy is highly susceptible to conditioning from pain and fear, NOT a stage where the puppy shows fear. The fear-imprint period, or fear period, is sometimes misused to excuse a puppy with a fearful temperament. Again, a puppy showing fear is not because of him being in the fear-imprint period.

Puppies that are not socialized during this period can develop a fearful temperament. There is a difference between temperament and behavior. According to W. Handel in his article, "The Psychological Basis of Temperament Testing," temperament is "the sum total of all inborn and acquired physical and mental traits and talents which determines, forms, and regulates behavior in the environment." So temperament is the trait; behavior is the action. For instance, a dog that has a fearful temperament may exhibit aggressive behavior such as barking or biting. The temperament is fearful, but the behavior exhibited is aggression.

It is very important not to make a big deal about things that scare your puppy. If something scares your puppy, you should do nothing. If something frightens your puppy, and you reassure him by petting and telling him it is all right, you are just reinforcing the fearfulness. You are in fact telling the puppy, "It is OK to be afraid, this is the behavior I want from you; good dog." If you chase after the puppy, become afraid for your puppy, and make a big fuss over him, he will become more fearful because of your reaction, not from the incident itself.

In a dog pack, when something occurs that frightens a member of the pack, the other dogs simply walk over, sniff the puppy or dog, and move on. They do not make a big deal about what happened. The way the dogs handle it enables the puppy or dog to move on, realizing, "Oh, no big deal."

Keep all training positive during this period. During this stage, you should never use rough corrections on your puppy; do not do anything that would make your puppy become fearful of you. Puppies at this age also have very short attention spans so keep all training sessions short. We will go into further detail on this subject in upcoming chapters.

During this stage of development, puppies are taking in a plethora of new information through their senses. Everything your puppy goes through during this stage is a learning experience, therefore a training opportunity. They are learning faster than at any other time in their life. Everything they come into contact with makes an impact on their brain. What they learn now, they will carry into their adult lives. How you handle your puppy during this stage will determine what kind of adult dog you will have. This is the best time to start teaching your puppy appropriate behaviors. You will hear us say this many times, and you need to make this your new mantra: **"Train early; train often,** because it *is easier to train good behaviors than undo bad behaviors."* This will be one of the more time-consuming developmental levels for you, the human. After all, just as with a human baby, your puppy depends on you for everything. If you put the time in, a trusting, stable, wonderful adult dog will forever reward you.

Adolescence: five to eighteen months

Adolescence can appear in smaller dogs as early as five months. In larger breeds, it can start as late as nine or ten months. In giant breeds, adolescence does not take place until twelve to eighteen months. In general, the larger the dog, the longer it will take to physically mature.

If you have or know a teenager, you know that adolescence is a difficult thing for parents to deal with. This is the same with puppy adolescence. As stated before, people often give up or surrender dogs to shelters around six to nine months of age. Most of these pups had no prior training or pack structure established from the beginning. Many of them are simply out of control. If you come across someone wanting to give you a six- to nine-month-old puppy, beware. Chances are it has had no previous training, and know that it will take a lot of work on your part to essentially rehabilitate this puppy. It can be done, but will be challenging and most likely will require a professional trainer to help. If you wait to train your puppy until it is six months old, you will have a much harder time than if you start from the beginning. Going through adolescence is much easier with a puppy that has had a stable training program from the beginning.

During this stage, puppies become more independent and will test the boundaries by not listening to previously learned commands and by wandering off and not coming when called. Males get a burst of testosterone around this time, which will lead to scent marking if not neutered. Females will go through estrus or the "heat" cycle, which lasts for three weeks. During this time, the female may become erratic in her behavior, and some can become aggressive. We recommend that people spay or neuter pets as soon as possible. As discussed before, with the pet overpopulation and all the knowledge needed to be a responsible breeder, there is no reason for a pet owner to keep a dog intact. Pets that are intact also have a higher incidence of cancer later in life.

During this stage of development, your puppy may also go through a second fear-imprint period. He may become shy or timid toward something familiar or afraid to approach new things. Do not reward the behavior by treating him while he is in a fearful state or by petting him and telling him it is OK. Reward when he approaches the situation and do not make too much fuss over it.

If you follow the Puppy Montessori program, you should not have any major second-fear issues in your puppy. That being said, every puppy is different, and each puppy has a different temperament, so do not be surprised if you experience this with your puppy. Keep it positive, and it will pass. The great thing about adolescence is that these dogs are athletic, full of energy, and a joy to play with. During this time, it is important to know that these phases pass, and now is the time to reinforce or step up previous training. Knowing that this stage is coming will help you understand why your puppy is doing what he is doing. Knowing is half the battle.

Chapter 3

Communication and Name Recognition

A dog can express more with his tail in seconds than his owner can express with his tongue in hours. ~Author Unknown

Animals use two types of communication.

- Intraspecific communication: communication between two or more individuals of the same species.
- Interspecific communication; communication between different species of animals.

We communicate with our puppy through interspecific communication. This means that we have to teach our puppy what our communication means, and in turn, we need to understand what its language means. Dogs communicate with us in many ways: verbally, through body language, with eye contact, etc. When you try to take a bone away from a dog, and he stares at you, curls his lips, and growls, he is communicating first through the stare (eye contact), then the curl of the lip (body language), and the growl (verbal) that if you push it, he will bite! Most people understand this and will not push the limit. This is interspecific communication, which does not need to be taught to us as adults. However, small children may be bitten by not understanding what the animal is trying to communicate. A small child needs to be told what this behavior means; otherwise, the child will learn quickly after being bitten. Other dogs automatically know what this communication means and will take heed, usually at the first glare. This is Intraspecific communication.

In the same way, in American culture, when humans greet each other, it is polite to make eye contact, smile, reach out your hand to shake the other's, or even hug the other person. All the humans understand this intraspecific communication. However, many people are bitten every year because they try to do the same to a dog. How many times have you seen people greet a strange dog by smiling, making eye contact, leaning forward, reaching out an arm, and talking in a high-pitched voice, only to end up getting bitten? Let us analyze this human approach. First, the smiling can be mistaken by the dog as a snarl. In dog language, eye contact and moving forward can be considered a challenge. The least threatening of these communications is the high-pitched voice, which can make some dogs excited. Therefore, an excited dog that misinterprets your approach as aggressive is likely to bite. Dogs have a way of greeting each other, and some may not understand that the human communication is a friendly one; they actually see it as a threat. During this time the dog most likely was giving nonverbal communications of his own that were simply missed by the human, such as ears back, tail tucked or held very high, and maybe he even looked away to avoid eye contact.

Therefore, you see why it is important to establish a common language and communication system between you and your dog. Do not assume that your puppy automatically knows what you are saying—a common mistake most people make.

Humans communicate mostly through verbal communication, whereas dogs use body language and cues to communicate. Most people talk too much to their puppy. By constantly talking to your puppy without ever establishing a common language, your puppy will not learn what the words mean and will appear to ignore you. The puppy is only ignoring you because the words mean nothing to him. We liken this to the teacher in the cartoon strip "Peanuts"; remember how she would say, "Wa, wa, wa, wa, wa"? This is what your puppy or dog hears every time you talk, unless you establish what the words mean. We have heard many people that say, "My dog never listens to me." We have also heard people say that dogs come with a set number of words they should know. To clear this up, puppies DO NOT come with a common set of human terms that they automatically know. They have to be taught. If you brought a wild animal into your home, such as a mountain lion, you would not expect it to understand anything you say to it; after all, it is a wild animal. In turn, we should not expect another animal even though domestic, to understand anything we say.

The quickest way to teach your puppy what your language means is to make ALL your words mean something. If you spoke to your puppy only when teaching it the language, he would quickly learn that everything you say has meaning and should be listened to. Now, we know this is not possible for most families. Children love to talk to the puppy, and we as humans like to talk to our dogs in loving ways that have nothing to do with teaching the puppy. However, you should keep in mind that the more you talk to your puppy—the more he might ignore you.

Naming your puppy is fun for the whole family. Many people name their puppy right away, and some people wait to see what the puppy's characteristics are going to be to pick a fitting name. However and whatever you choose to name your puppy, the important part comes in teaching the puppy that this "name" means him. Many people do not realize that you need to teach your puppy his name. Through the years, we have seen puppies that do not respond to their name or any other command simply because the human language was not properly established with the dog. This commonly occurs in families with lots of children, where everyone is constantly talking to the puppy but no one has established what the words mean. Some puppies will learn their name over time without being "taught"; however, teaching your puppy his name early will create a puppy that is more responsive to that name.

Name recognition is one of the first things you should teach your puppy. Along with name recognition, we will teach the term "good." Contrary to popular belief, dogs do not automatically know what "good" means unless you teach them. When we say our puppy's name, our goal is to get him to look at us so we can give another command such as come, sit, stay, etc. It is the foundation of getting your puppy to pay attention to you.

 ALERT! Never—and we mean never—use your puppy's name in a negative way, such as to scold him. By using your puppy's name negatively, you will create a dog that either ignores his name or will run away when his name is called.

Remember, in a dog pack, dogs do not have a given name. Each dog in the pack is known for its position or hierarchy in the pack. The energy of each individual dog gives him the appointed status in the pack.

To a dog, the name is just a word, a word that has an association either negative or positive. We have seen dogs that had such a negative association with their name that the name had to be changed. Dogs learn all words by association. If every time I look at my dog, say the word "Max," and give him a treat, he develops a positive association with that word and will look at me every time I say "Max." On the other hand, if I yell the word "MAX!" in a stern voice and when the puppy looks at me, I grab him and rub his nose in urine, the word "Max" takes on a negative association. The next time I say "Max" he will not be as interested in coming to me and may run away. In turn, if everyone in the house is constantly saying, "Max, Max, Max," and there is no association either positively or negatively, the dog will fail to know that the word "Max" means anything. Dogs do not automatically know that a name means who they are; they have to be taught with name recognition. Name recognition helps the dog associate the word "Max" with who they are. So, how do we teach a puppy what his name means? We do this through positive reinforcement.

For this process you will need a treat pouch which hooks onto your pants and some treats. Treat pouches come in many shapes and sizes and you can purchase them online or at local pet stores or through our website, www.supermutts.com

Treat pouch   Natural balance beef roll

 NOTE: *The treats you use should be something small, very tasty, easy to chew, and should be moist so your puppy does not have to drink water right after eating them. We highly recommend Natural Balance food roll cut into tiny pieces for all our training needs. Natural Balance food roll comes in many different flavors (e.g., beef, chicken, lamb, etc.) and is a complete nutrition, so you can substitute it for some of the puppy's regular diet. You can purchase it through our website at* www.supermutts.com *For a more inexpensive treat you can use low fat turkey hot dogs, cut into small pieces; however, these are not a complete nutrition and cannot be used to substitute regular feedings. Too many can upset the puppy's stomach.*

To teach your puppy his name, have your treat pouch handy, show your puppy the treats in your hand to let him know you have them. Give the puppy a treat. When your puppy looks up at you for another treat, say his name and give him a treat. Do this several times.

 ALERT! It is important to say the name only ONCE before giving the treat. You do not need to repeat the name; this will confuse the puppy and may hinder the learning process.

After you have done the above activity several times, you are ready to test your training. Wait until your puppy is not looking at you any longer and say his name, only once. If he looks at you, and AS SOON as he looks at you, give him a treat.

Repeat this exercise several times throughout the day in many different areas of your home and yard. Once your puppy is looking at you every time you say his name, then you can add the word "good."

Say your puppy's name. When he looks at you, say "good" and treat. Do this every time you say your puppy's name and he looks at you. You are now teaching your puppy what the term "good" means. "Good" means a treat is coming and the puppy will have a "good" association with the word.

Remember to say the name only once and say "good" only once. Do not repeat it over and over.

NOTE: *If your puppy does not look at you when you say the name, you may have moved ahead too quickly. You will need to start from the beginning, showing him the treats first, and saying his name.*

You will see that most puppies learn name recognition very quickly and will start looking at you immediately after you say the name.

Engagement

In teaching name recognition, you are also teaching what professional trainers call "engagement." Engagement simply means that the puppy "engages" with you regardless of what else is going on. The most common thing we see with dogs that come through our boarding school is lack of engagement with the human. The dog has learned that the rest of the world is more exciting and entertaining than the human. They have been given no reason to "engage" with their owners. Another reason for this is that the dogs do not see the owners as leaders. A dog will not pay attention on demand unless it sees you as the leader. By following the Puppy Montessori program, you are teaching engagement. Through name recognition, tethering, obedience, and leash work, you are teaching your puppy to engage with you.

Chapter 4 The Nursery

There is nothing so terrible in life that a sleeping puppy cannot conjure a smile ~Georgia Cameron

As we stated before, just as you prepare your home for a new baby, you must prepare it for your new baby dog. Setting up a nursery is one of, if not THE most important thing you can do for your new puppy. The nursery is essential, and the Puppy Montessori program does not work without it. The good news is you do not have to devote a whole room to a puppy nursery like you would a baby's nursery. You just need an area of a room to set it up. This space should be in an area of your home where you and your family spend most of your time, such as a family room. If your home is large, and you spend more time in one room than others at different times of the day (e.g., in a home office during the day and the family room in the evening), set up several nurseries around your home. For most people, however, one is sufficient. We want the puppy to be a part of our family and this will allow just that. The nursery will let your puppy see what is going on within the safety of the nursery.

The reason the nursery is such an important part of the program is that it allows you to have control over your puppy's freedom. By controlling your puppy's freedom, you can keep your puppy out of harm's way. It will also keep your carpet, furniture, shoes, clothing, pillows, etc., from being destroyed. Remember, **"It is easier to train good behaviors than undo**

bad ones." If you never allow your puppy to chew on these objects, he simply never will.

Never allow your puppy free reign of the house unsupervised. This is where most people make the biggest mistake. Many people bring a puppy home and let it have free reign of the house. This is the **number one** mistake made by pet parents. Too much freedom too soon is not good for you, your household, and especially not good for your puppy. Many people assume that their puppy will just figure it out. This never happens and will never happen. What happens is that people get frustrated and the puppy is punished for being a puppy. This creates a lack of trust for the owner, and the owner will spend a lot of time breaking bad behaviors. Many of these puppies are banished to the backyard, turned over to a shelter, or rehomed.

Another reason the nursery is important is that it is portable; you can move it from room to room. If you go on vacation with your puppy or to a friend's house for dinner, you can take the nursery with you. This provides a safe place for your puppy that is familiar to him no matter where you go. You can think of it as a playpen for your puppy.

The Puppy Montessori program teaches you to be proactive instead of reactive. It all starts with the nursery.

The nursery consists of:

- a four-by-four-foot ex pen, which becomes the nursery
- a small kennel
- A piece of sealed wallboard cut to four-by-four feet or slightly larger for the floor of the nursery.
- It should also include toys, a hard chew toy, bedding for the kennel, and food and water bowls.

You can find these items except the wallboard at your local pet store or can purchase them through our website at http:/www.supermutts.com

You will need to purchase the wallboard at a local home improvement store. It comes in four-by-eight-foot sheets, and most stores will cut it for you to the four-by-four size. Here is what your nursery should look like.

To assemble the nursery, place the sealed wallboard on the floor. Put the ex pen on top of the wallboard in a square, place the kennel inside the four-by-four area along with toys, chews, and a water bowl.

The sealed wallboard is to protect your own flooring from becoming soiled if the puppy does have an accident inside the nursery. If you have carpet, the wallboard is a must. Even if you put the nursery on a hard surface, you will still want to use the wallboard as the floor to your nursery. The sealed wallboard is extremely easy to clean, and if your puppy soils on your floor, he may continue to soil in that area after you remove the nursery because of any odor left behind after cleaning

 Alert! It is important to place the nursery away from walls, furniture, or anything your puppy can reach through the bars of the nursery.

Many people want to use the kitchen or bathroom or other tiled area of a home. We do not recommend this for two reasons.

1) It provides too much space in which your pet can either eliminate in or chew baseboards, electrical outlets, or other items.
2) The nursery is portable and you can move it to whatever room the family is in, thereby preventing the puppy from feeling isolated.

The small kennel inside the nursery is a necessity. A puppy that is successfully kennel trained is a blessing for several reasons. The kennel allows you to successfully potty train your puppy in the shortest amount of time. Dogs are den animals and like the security of a confined space. The kennel provides your pet with a comfortable place to sleep and provides the safety and security similar to that of a den they would provide for themselves in the wild.

Kennel training your pet also helps prevent separation anxiety in that it teaches your pet to be calm when left alone. Kennel training also sets your dog up to be comfortable whenever and wherever he may be in a kennel, such as at the groomer, at the veterinarian, during an emergency, or while traveling in the car. You can leave your pet alone and know that you will not come home to a destroyed house. You have a safe place to put your pet during a party or when you have guests over. You can leave the kennel open and the dog will choose to go in and sleep on his own when he needs alone time.

We know there are many people who are against kennel training their dog. These people are not pet professionals, and they are wrong. Period. Actually, one of the worst things you can do for your dog is NOT kennel train him. Pet professionals highly recommend kennel training your dog.

- The primary use for a crate/kennel is housetraining. Dogs do not like to soil their dens.
- The crate/kennel can limit access to the rest of the house while he learns other rules, like not to chew on furniture.
- Crates/kennels are a safe way to transport your dog in the car.

The Humane Society of the United States says this about crate training:

"Private room with a view. Ideal for traveling dogs or for those who just want a secure, quiet place to hang out at home—that is how your dog might describe his crate. It's his own personal den where he can find comfort and solitude while you know he's safe and secure—and not shredding your house while you're out running errands."

Crate training uses a dog's natural instincts as a den animal. A wild dog's den is his home, a place to sleep, hide from danger, and raise a family. The crate becomes your dog's den, an ideal spot to snooze or take refuge during a thunderstorm. All the puppies we have trained with the Puppy Montessori nursery program go into their kennels on their own to sleep, play, or just hang out.

Many of the problems that dogs develop come from people humanizing them. The first mistake people make is thinking that being in a kennel is like a person being in jail. This is incorrect thinking. They clearly do not understand the fact that dogs are "den" animals. This thinking often comes from many of the commercials on television that show pathetic dogs in puppy mills in wire-bottom kennels. Proper kennel training is nothing like that. Remember, we have to be the best surrogate dog parents we can be, and dog parents provide a den for their babies.

Oftentimes people believe kennels are bad because they or someone they know adopted an adult dog that had never been in a kennel. They put the dog in a kennel, left for work for eight hours, only to come home to a dog that destroyed the kennel, eliminated in it, and potentially chewed through it to the point of injuring itself. This is not because kennels are bad. It is because the human was ignorant. Whenever you aquire an adult dog that you know nothing about, you need to kennel train the dog before you leave it for eight hours alone in something it is unfamiliar with. This is why it is extremely important to kennel train your new puppy. Puppies get used to a kennel fairly quickly. In fact, depending on where you aquire your puppy, the job may already be done.

Now, we will say that kennel training does not entail leaving a puppy in a kennel 24-7; people can misuse the kennel. A puppy also cannot be left in a kennel or the nursery for eight hours alone while you are at work. **The kennel or nursery should NEVER be used as punishment.**

There are proper ways to kennel your dog to ensure your dog will thrive and be a very happy, well-adjusted dog. The dog sees the kennel as his den and actually needs this space. You need to see it as his bedroom.

There are many types of kennels on the market. Whichever one you choose should have a solid bottom, not a wire bottom, and should be only large enough for your puppy to stand up, turn around, and stretch out while lying down. You may think, "larger is better," but not in the eyes of your puppy. A large kennel that is too big for your pet may make him feel insecure, dogs like the security of a smaller kennel. If the kennel is too large, the puppy will sleep in one end and eliminate in the other; this defeats the potty training process.

There are two types of kennels that we recommend for the nursery setup. For smaller puppies, such as Shih-Tzus, Yorkies, toy poodles, etc., we recommend using a small plastic Vari Kennel. For larger puppies, we recommend using a kennel such as the MidWest kennels. Each comes in a variety of sizes. It is really a matter of preference. Here are photos of both:

Vari Kennel   MidWest kennel

The MidWest kennels come with one door or two. You can use whichever one you prefer for the nursery setup. You should put a blanket or some form of bedding inside the kennel for your puppy to snuggle in.

Now that you have your nursery set up, let us get started on the program!

Chapter 5 Potty Training

When a puppy takes fifty catnaps in the course of the day, he cannot always be expected to sleep the night through. ~Albert Payson Terhune

How to potty train or house train a puppy is one of our most frequently asked questions from new puppy owners. It is a large source of frustration for most puppy parents but if done correctly, can be a very simple process. There is no set number of days or weeks it will take to potty train your puppy. However, we have known of puppies that are house trained in less than one week, using this potty training program. Each puppy is different in that it will take some longer than others. It is important to know that you cannot rush this process, and there are no shortcuts. The key is to stick to the program and be consistent.

The nursery is for young puppies, ages eight weeks to six months. The primary reason for the kennel inside the nursery is potty training. Since most puppies do not like to soil where they sleep, one of the purposes of the kennel is to teach the puppy to hold his bladder for longer and longer periods of time.

The primary reason for the nursery is for controlling your puppy's freedom when he cannot be supervised. It is important for you to know that during the potty training process, your puppy can NEVER be left unsupervised until you know he is 100 percent potty trained.

 NOTE: *The number one reason contributing to potty training problems is giving a puppy too much unsupervised freedom before it is fully potty trained. In fact, the number one reason most people have any kind of problems with their puppies is too much freedom too soon.*

Puppies eliminate frequently; they do not understand or know where the appropriate place is to do so. It is our job as pet parents to teach them. If you allow your puppy to make a mistake and eliminate in the house, you are setting the process back and confusing the dog. It will take twice as long to potty train your puppy if you allow this to happen.

The potty training process is the most time-consuming aspect of owning a puppy. Depending on how often your puppy eliminates, you may be taking him out as much as every thirty minutes in the beginning. If you are unable to devote this kind of time to the process, you may want to ask friends or relatives to help. If you work, and do not have anyone to assist you, then you will have to send your puppy to a doggie day care that understands and will work on the potty training process.

Other things that contribute to housetraining problems are free feeding and using paper or puppy potty pads for training.

Free feeding means leaving a bowl of food down all the time for the puppy to eat at random. It also means that you cannot time when your puppy needs to eliminate. It is much easier to house train a dog when you can predict when it will need to eliminate. The way to do that is to control feeding times. We suggest keeping a diary to record a dog's eating and elimination times. This approach can help you recognize patterns the dog has formed. Once you have developed a pattern, it will be easier to take the dog out at certain intervals. Each puppy is different, but the average puppy or dog eliminates twenty minutes after eating.

One problem with training to paper or potty pads is that a dog sometimes begins to generalize about the paper or potty pad. For instance, a dog may think it can go anywhere as long as it is in the room with the paper. Sometimes the dog will generalize to a nearby throw rug. The dog has generalized going indoors on paper to going on another item with a similar shape. The dog may even generalize to the entire room or to the entire indoor area. By using potty pads, you are telling your puppy it is OK to eliminate indoors. We do not recommend training using potty pads.

During the potty training process, your puppy will cycle through one of four areas throughout the day:

- the kennel
- outside to eliminate
- supervised free time/playtime in the house
- the nursery

The potty training process and the kennel training process go hand in hand for new puppies. How your puppy responds to both depends on his temperament (dominant or submissive) how he was raised by the breeder, and his age.

When you bring your puppy home for the first time, he should be given time outdoors in a designated area to relieve himself. Do this with him on leash. When you bring your puppy indoors, the nursery should be set up. The puppy is not given any free time in the house at all but should be taken to the nursery.

 NOTE: *We know that bringing a new puppy into the home is exciting, and that you and your family will want to play with the puppy right away. However, there are designated times to play with the puppy and when you first come home is not one of them.*

The way you introduce your puppy, from the moment you bring him home, sets the stage for how the puppy sees you and your family in terms of pack structure. We will go into further detail on pack structure in Chapter 15.

Keep in mind that everything you do with your puppy from this moment on, is teaching him how to be. Remember, **"It is easier to train good behaviors than to undo bad ones!"**

Introduce your puppy to the kennel by showing him a treat, then toss a treat or two inside the kennel and let him go in on his own. The kennel should have bedding, a toy, and a chew bone inside. Let him explore inside the kennel without shutting the door. Let him come out of the kennel on his own. Toss a treat in and let him go into the kennel again. Do this several times. This will teach him that going into the kennel makes good things happen. Once he is going in and out regularly, you can add a word later such as "kennel" or "crate"; this will allow you to give a one-word command, and your puppy will go into the kennel.

After several times of your puppy going in and out of the kennel, you will then close the door once he goes into the kennel. Let him stay there for a few minutes, and **if he is quiet,** let him out again. Do this several times. Once the puppy is going in easily and is quiet, let him stay in his kennel for thirty minutes.

 NOTE: *Some puppies may cry at first if they are older puppies or have not been used to confinement. This is usually short-lived. It is **extremely** important not to respond to the crying. **DO NOT** look at the puppy, talk to the puppy, yell at the puppy, etc. Make sure your children understand this principle as well. No one can give the puppy any attention at this time. Your puppy will quiet down once he realizes it is not getting him anywhere.*

 ALERT! If you give your puppy any attention at all during this time, or if you do the worst possible thing and let him out of the kennel, you have just taught him that crying gets him what he wants, and he will continue doing so. You are TEACHING your puppy to cry. You are also teaching your puppy that he is the leader, in that he can control you by whining or crying. This sets the stage for leadership problems later in life. Give

your puppy attention or let him out of his kennel only when he is quiet.

People who let their puppy out during this time are the ones that develop adult dogs that have problems with kennels—e.g., crying, whining, chewing, and escaping. They actually teach the puppy that confinement is bad. **Do not be one of those people**. Let your puppy out of the kennel only when he is quiet. This will teach your puppy that "quiet" is what gets him out of the kennel. This also teaches your puppy self-control and that you are the leader; you tell him when he can come out of the kennel—he does not tell you.

Once he is quiet, you can toss a few more treats into the kennel to reassure him that the kennel brings good things.

 NOTE: *Sometimes giving attention right away when the puppy quiets down will cause him to start crying again. You will have to judge if your puppy is one of those puppies. If he is, then do not disturb him once he quiets down.*

Once your puppy quiets down, let him stay in the kennel for thirty minutes before taking him outside to eliminate. If your puppy falls asleep during this time, let him remain in the kennel until he awakens. This requires attention on your part, because as soon as you notice him awaken, you need to open the kennel and take him immediately outside.

 NOTE: *Puppies generally eliminate upon wakening, after eating, and after play. Smaller puppies, such as Chihuahuas or Yorkshire terriers, need to eliminate more frequently because of their small bladder size.*

With your puppy on a leash, take him outside to eliminate in a designated area. Do not play with your puppy or talk to him at this time. Puppies have very short attention spans and if you distract them, they will not eliminate. Walk around with your puppy until he eliminates. Once he urinates, you can then give him a lot of praise, pets, a treat, and say good boy or girl. Make a big deal of it but not so much that you scare your puppy. Some puppies will stop eliminating when you praise. If your puppy is one of these puppies, you will need to wait until immediately after he finishes eliminating to give praise.

It is important not to go inside too soon, some puppies will need to urinate or defecate more than once so give your puppy adequate time after he eliminates to potentially go again. Every time he eliminates, give the same praise and treat to let him know he did something good.

After you are sure your puppy is done eliminating, take him in the house. At this time, you have two options. You can give your puppy free time with the family—on leash, tethered to you—or you can give him free time in the nursery. We recommend free time with the family as much as possible.

 NOTE: *Use the nursery for those times when you are too busy to keep an eye on the puppy, he has eliminated outside, and he still needs free time out of his kennel. This might be in the morning, when you and your family are getting ready to go to work or school, etc. This is where the nursery is your best friend. Keep the kennel door open so he can go in to rest if needed and have toys for him to play with. This will keep your puppy safe and out of trouble when you cannot keep an eye on him.*

At first, you will give only about thirty minutes of playtime or nursery time; then your puppy should go back to the kennel. After thirty minutes to one hour in the kennel, take him back outside to potty. You will do this rotation throughout the day.

If your puppy does not eliminate outside, then he goes back to his kennel for another thirty minutes.

 ALERT! If you allow free time in the house when your puppy did not eliminate outside, we promise you he WILL go in the house. You have just set the stage for teaching your puppy to eliminate in the house. You have made THE biggest potty training mistake. Do not do that!

Remember: It is easier to train good behaviors than undo bad ones!

Eventually you will extend the rotation time to one hour, then two hours, then four hours, etc. You need to keep track of how often your puppy eliminates and time your outings accordingly. For instance, if you rotate through several thirty-minute sessions of kennel, outside, kennel, etc., and your puppy eliminates only on the fourth time out, then you can extend the time indoors to two hours. Each puppy will be different. This is where a diary will come in handy to track your puppy's elimination habits.

 NOTE: *Sometimes after play, puppies need to eliminate, if you find your puppy is one of those puppies, you will need to take him outside to potty after the play session and before putting him back in his kennel.*

If your puppy is getting confused and eliminating in his crate or nursery or during playtime, then you should step up the intervals to every fifteen minutes (e.g., fifteen minutes in the crate, then outdoors to potty. If your pet potties outdoors, he gets fifteen minutes of free time in the house or nursery, then outside to potty. If no elimination occurs, then back to the crate for fifteen minutes). Once it appears your pet is catching on, and eliminating outside during these intervals, then you can lengthen the time in the crate to thirty minutes, one hour, then two hours, etc. The key is to extend the length of time between potty breaks; this teaches your puppy bladder control.

It is imperative that you go out with your dog EVERY TIME he is to eliminate until he is successful for several months. You are marking the behavior by praising the puppy every time he goes outside so you must be with him to do so. This is part of the training process.

 ALERT! If you catch your dog in the act of eliminating indoors, clap your hands or say NO in a stern voice to interrupt the process, and take him outdoors to finish eliminating. If he finishes eliminating outdoors, praise and treat. Do not spank, slap, or rub his nose in his mess, as this will not solve the problem and will only make him fearful of you.

> **If you find your puppy eliminated when you were not watching, slap your own hand for not paying attention, and simply clean up the mess. DO NOT scold your puppy; he will not know why you are scolding him. He will think you are scolding him for what he is doing at that moment, not what he did five or ten minutes ago.**

Once your puppy is eliminating outside consistently, you can start using a word every time he goes, such as "go potty" or "potty." The puppy will start to associate that word with the act of eliminating. In the future, you can use the word to have your puppy eliminate on command. This is very helpful when time is of the essence, and you need to have your puppy eliminate quickly without dillydallying around—for instance, in inclement weather, when traveling, etc. We have all seen people standing in the rain or snow for long periods with a dog that is taking its time to eliminate because the ground is wet. If you have a command to give your dog, he will go quickly, and you will not have to stand in the rain or possibly have a dog that will eliminate indoors because he did not go outside.

Teaching the "go potty" command

To teach the "go potty" command, you must wait until your puppy is in the act of eliminating before you give the command. You do not give the command before the puppy has learned what the command means. You must teach the command first. When your puppy is in the act of eliminating, say, "Go potty," "good," and treat. The next time he eliminates, say, "Go potty," "good," and treat. Do this several times, every time your puppy eliminates outside. Eventually, when your puppy starts to give the sign he is about to eliminate (sniffing the ground, circling), you will say, "Go potty," right before he eliminates. Repeat several times. Eventually you will give the command, "Go potty," and your puppy will go on command. This is when you know your puppy has learned what the command means. If you give the command, "Go potty," and your puppy does not go, he has not learned what the command means. You must go back to giving the command while he is in the act of eliminating until he learns what the command means.

It is important not to continually repeat the command. When teaching and when giving the "go potty" command, say the command only once. Never give the go potty command before the puppy eliminates if you have not taught him what the command means. We have all seen people who stand in front of a dog, repeating the command, "Go potty, go potty, go potty," while the dog is ignoring them. They clearly never taught the dog what "go potty" means by doing the initial training. Repeating a command that a dog does not clearly understand only teaches the dog that your words mean nothing. Your dog cannot do what he clearly does not understand.

In summary, consistency, timing, and follow-through are the keys to any training program. The goal is to set your pet up for success not failure. Even though it can be a time-consuming process, if you follow this simple plan, you can successfully potty train your dog in the shortest amount of time.

Chapter 6

Socialization

The reason a dog has so many friends is that he wags his tail instead of his tongue. ~ Unknown

Kennel training and proper socialization are the two most important things you can do for your puppy. One is equally as important as the other in growing a stable dog.

Socialization is something that you will continue throughout your puppy's life. Many—and we would go so far as to say most—behavioral problems in adult dogs are because of improper puppy socialization. Puppies that are not socialized properly can develop fear, aggression, and anxiety.

Tools needed for socialization are a six-foot leash, treat pouch, and treats. The leash should be either nylon or leather. We do not recommend chain leashes or retractable leashes.

treat pouch   leather lead

Many years ago, puppy owners were told they needed to keep their puppy isolated until all the vaccinations were up to date. The problem with this thinking is that the puppy is never exposed to the outside world during the critical stage (eight to sixteen weeks). Some veterinarians still tell puppy owners to isolate their puppy during this time, but most are moving away from this thinking. Many clients contact us because of problems of fear or aggression, only for us to discover that they have not socialized their puppy outside the home, because the puppy was not fully vaccinated.

The realization today is that the risk of a puppy developing major behavioral issues by isolating it far outweighs the risk of it contracting a fatal disease if you socialize the puppy. This being said, you need to be smart about how you socialize your puppy. You do not want to take your puppy to places that have dogs with questionable health, such as dog parks, shelters, or adoption events. But you still need to socialize your puppy. You also want to keep all interactions positive and not force your puppy or cause him to become fearful during the socialization process.

You can take your puppy with you and carry it in your arms to the bank, the hardware store, pet stores, etc. Let people pet the puppy, let children pet the puppy, sit with the puppy in a busy parking lot with cars going by. Take the puppy outside during thunderstorms, and make it a positive experience by playing with toys. Get your puppy signed up for a reputable doggie day care that will responsibly socialize your puppy with vaccinated dogs of all sizes and ages. Get your puppy around other dogs and with cats if possible. If your puppy is one that needs grooming, schedule the grooming appointment as soon as possible with a groomer that understands how to handle young puppies. The important thing is not to isolate your puppy at all. Socialize it to as many different areas, sights, sounds, and surfaces as possible. As stated before, keep all these social activities positive so as not to frighten the puppy.

While we say to socialize your puppy to many different situations, you also need to control those social interactions. You should always have your treat pouch with you, and you should always have your puppy engage with you during these outings. You do not want to let your puppy pull you on the leash to every person it sees and jump on them. You do not want your puppy to do anything you would not want it to do when it is an adult. You should always bring your puppy to the people or situations—not let your puppy bring you. Always have treats with you while introducing your puppy to new people or situations. Once you introduce your puppy to people, coax your puppy to you with the treats and reward him for paying attention to you. This teaches the puppy that even though there are distractions around, he still needs to pay attention to you. If your puppy gets overly excited and wants to pull and jump on people, you need to tell the people to ignore the puppy until he is calm. Get his attention with treats and a lot of praise. He needs to know that following you is fun. Always end the session with your puppy engaged with you.

 ALERT! Never—and we mean never—allow people to pet and coo over your puppy if he is jumping up on them. Doing so is rewarding your puppy for the behavior and telling your puppy it is OK to jump up on people. What your puppy does now, he will do as an adult. If you cannot control the people in the environment, then you should create situations with people who will listen to your instruction. You can also put a vest on the puppy that says, "Puppy in training, please ignore." Remember our motto: "It is easier to train good behaviors than undo bad ones."

Socialization begins as soon as you bring your puppy home. How your family interacts with the puppy is very important, and it is the first unfamiliar social situation your puppy will be in. All family members need to follow the same rules for the puppy. In fact, it is good to make a written schedule for your family to follow regarding your puppy. For instance, potty schedule, playtimes, who is responsible for tasks such as feeding and potty training, etc. Socialization begins with everyone in your home, including other pets.

Socialization with children:

People with small children should not allow the child to pull, hit, slap, or play roughly with the puppy. Tell children to ignore the puppy when it is in the nursery or kennel. If a child stands at the nursery and harasses the puppy, it will teach him to bark, jump up on the kennel, whine, etc.

 NOTE: *The puppy's nursery is his "quiet" place to rest or play on his own. You should teach your children to respect the puppy's nursery time and ignore the puppy at this time.*

Children should not play with the puppy in a way that makes the puppy jump up on them. Family members should never play roughly or use their hands to wrestle with the puppy. Remember, puppies have sharp claws and teeth that can injure a small child. If a puppy is encouraged to jump up or chew on a child, the puppy is learning to jump up and chew on all children and will continue to do so in the future, not only to your children but also to children that may visit your home. **Remember, it is easier to train good behaviors than undo bad ones!** It is important that an adult take full responsibility for how the puppy interacts with children and teach the children how to properly interact with the puppy.

It is important that when your puppy is out of his nursery for free time with the family, he is on leash. The leash allows you to keep an eye on your puppy and control the interactions that the puppy has with people, children, and other pets.

Socialization in home

During the time out of the nursery, do not allow your puppy to roam around the house freely. You will control this with the leash. If you go to other rooms of your house, the puppy will go with you on leash. This teaches the puppy that he does not own the house; the house is yours, and you control the comings and goings. It in fact teaches the puppy that you are the leader. He follows you—you do not follow him. This sets the stage for building a leader/follower relationship. While your puppy is on leash, you should not allow your puppy to pull you or any family member to what he wants. You should always guide the puppy, using treats and praise when he pays attention to you.

 NOTE: *Remember to have your treat pouch on at all times that you are interacting with or socializing your puppy. You should never take your puppy out of the nursery or kennel without having your treat pouch and your leash. You should also always have approved chew toys available.*

Leash Desensitization

Some puppies will "pull back" on the leash the first few times they encounter it and may attempt to chew the leash. These puppies will need to be "desensitized" to the leash. Start by connecting the leash to your puppy's collar and let him drag it around. Reward your puppy with a treat for paying attention to you when the leash is on. Eventually pick up the leash and start to walk forward, encouraging the puppy to follow, keeping the treats in your hand, and letting him smell them. Once the puppy takes a step forward—and ONLY when he steps forward—say, "Good," and give him a treat. The more steps he takes, the more times you give the word "good" and a treat. Do this several times a day for five minutes at a time until he is following you regularly.

 ALERT! You should never pull the puppy or scold the puppy for pulling back on the leash, and you should never pick the puppy up and carry him when he does this behavior.

By scolding the puppy or pulling the puppy, you will create a fear of the leash or a "negative association" to the leash. By picking him up and carrying him, you have rewarded the behavior, and he will continue to pull back in the future. It is important to keep a loose leash.

Picture of puppy pulling back on leash

By using this method of praise and treat, you will see that puppies quickly learn to follow you on the leash and are more than willing to follow you, even off leash.

The leash allows you to control how your puppy interacts with other family members. If your puppy tries to jump up on people, you can control him with the leash by stepping on the leash or simply giving a small tug and saying "no" or "aghh, aghh."

The leash keeps your puppy from being able to chew on tables, shoes, pillows, etc. If your puppy tries to chew on these objects, the leash gives you the ability to correct the behavior and redirect the puppy to an approved chew toy. It also teaches the puppy that when on leash, he is to follow the human. This will eliminate pulling problems in the future. Puppies are natural followers, as are all young mammals. Look to nature and you will see that bear cubs, wolf cubs, lion cubs, and others all follow the mother. The mother does not follow the baby.

By using the leash, you will quickly see that young puppies take direction very well and rapidly learn what is acceptable and what is not. The key is to be consistent. If you are not paying attention and you let your puppy chew on an unapproved item such as a table leg, shoe, leash, etc., rest assured he will chew on it again. The key is to catch the puppy the moment he goes for the unapproved object and redirect him to an approved toy. Once he understands what is approved and what is not, he will cease to do the unapproved behavior. It is that simple.

If you do not want to keep your puppy tethered to you at all times, you can use the leash as a dragline. A dragline simply means that you leave the leash on the puppy to "drag" around. Use this only when you are able to keep a close eye on the puppy and keep him confined to the room you are in, such as when you are sitting down at the end of the day to watch some television. Never leave a dragline on a puppy that you cannot watch at all times. The dragline allows you to get to your puppy quickly if needed. You can step on the dragline if he tries to run away, or you can pick it up if your puppy needs some redirection.

Socialization to other pets

When introducing your new puppy to other animals in your family, the leash and nursery are very important tools. For initial meetings, your puppy should be in the nursery, with the other pets outside the nursery. Any dogs or cats in your family can sniff the puppy through the nursery without causing harm to each other. This gives you a way to monitor how your other pets and your new puppy will respond to each other.

Once you have established that your pets are OK with the new puppy, you can introduce them, with the puppy on leash. If you are unsure of how your dogs will respond to the puppy, they also should be on leash.

By controlling your new puppy with a leash in front of your other pets, you are teaching the puppy what is acceptable behavior and teaching your other pets that you are the leader and are in control of the new puppy. You should never allow your other pets to attack or act overly assertive to the new puppy, and you should never allow your new puppy to act overly assertive toward them. You should always control the interactions and never let them "work it out" on their own.

 ALERT! Be aware that your puppy's energy level may be far greater than that of older or senior pets in your home. It is up to you to control the interaction and not let the puppy control or dominate your other pets.

Case Study:

Before we became dog trainers, we acquired a pit bull puppy. We had two other adult dogs at the time, a five-year-old Dalmatian and a two-year-old ridgeback mix. We loved our new puppy and wanted to get her off on the right start, so we enrolled her in a puppy class at a mega pet store as soon as possible. She excelled in class, learned her obedience quickly, and was the star of the class. We were so proud. We had noticed that she would act aggressively toward our Dalmatian upon coming out of the crate or from behind a door. When they played, we noticed scratches and wounds on the puppy that seemed to indicate more than just play. We discussed this with the trainer of the puppy class. Her advice to us was that most scuffles with dogs sound worse than they are, and we should just let them "work it out." We thought that since she was a trainer, we should do what she said, despite our concern.

The first bad fight occurred when the pit bull was only twelve to sixteen weeks old. She went after the Dalmatian, and he had enough. A fight ensued and the puppy ended up at the vet with a drain put in her head. Several more fights between her and the Dalmatian and the Ridgeback led us to hire a trainer to come into our home.

He explained that letting a pit bull and other large dogs "work it out" was wrong advice. He put a training plan in place that helped establish us as the leaders of the pack. It worked for a while, but the fights became worse and more frequent the older she got. We consulted a dog behaviorist and came to realize that the pit bull we acquired was "hard wired" to fight other dogs, period. Had we understood this and handled things differently when she was a puppy, we may have been able to avert the fighting by starting a leadership program much sooner. By the time we allowed her to begin fighting, it was too late. The inexperienced trainer had given us bad advice about just letting them "work it out." Unfortunately the sad ending to this story is that we had to euthanize her. Although she became a very well trained dog, her dog aggression was an innate temperament that no amount of training would change. This dog is the reason we became professional dog trainers; we wanted to understand more about dogs and give the right advice when people asked us.

Therefore, if someone tells you to let your older dog and your new puppy just "work it out," you need to find a new resource. That is bad advice, period.

You should allow your other dogs and your puppy to play, but only when supervised, and the puppy should always be on leash. If you feel that either pet is becoming overly assertive, you can stop the play. Dogs play to establish dominance and pack hierarchy. You should not scold your older dog if he "corrects" the puppy for playing too roughly. Older dogs will teach puppies what is appropriate play and what is not. For instance, two dogs are playing. Your puppy bites a little too hard, and the older dog lunges out and gives a quick bite to the puppy. The puppy backs down, submits, and it is over. You should never correct your older dog for doing this. This is how your older dog establishes his dominance and maintains bite inhibition of the puppy. These are normal dominance rituals that occur in every dog pack.

If your current dog is a submissive one and lets the puppy act overly assertive, or bully it, you should control your puppy with the leash. Allow your puppy to play, but do not allow it to get out of control. You should redirect the puppy's attention to an approved toy or chew. You can also remove your puppy to the nursery if his behavior is overly assertive with your other pets.

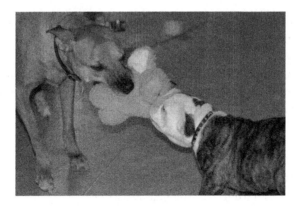

Normal play between puppy and adult dog

Besides socializing your new puppy with your current pets, you also need to socialize him with other dogs in general. For a puppy that is going to be an "only dog" in the household, it is imperative to socialize him on a regular basis with other dogs. Let's face it, we are not dogs. We can only do so much to communicate with our dogs. Dogs speak dog. We believe that dogs need that routine mingling with others of their own species. We have seen many issues related to the fact that a dog was in an "only dog" household and only around humans. These dogs forget how to be "a dog" when in the company of other dogs. It is a sad thing to witness. They become clingy to humans and aggressive or fearful of other dogs.

A great place to start socializing with other dogs is a puppy class. Puppy classes allow you to socialize your puppy with other puppies in a structured environment. To find a good puppy class, consult with your veterinarian or other pet professionals in your area. You can also check with the AKC for a STAR Puppy Class in your area. "STAR" stands for "socialization, training, activity, and responsibility." See appendix A for the AKC website.

You should also look for a dog day care facility that will socialize your puppy in a structured environment with dogs of all sizes. The facility should have trainers on staff that understand puppy socialization and keep a controlled environment for all dogs in their care.

 ALERT! We do not recommend socializing your puppy at dog parks. Yes, there are plenty of dogs of all sizes at dog parks; however, most of the dogs at dog parks are out of control. A dog park has the potential to become a terrible experience for your new puppy. If you go to a dog park and another dog attacks or mauls your puppy, it can create a puppy that becomes fearful of other dogs or dog aggressive.

All socialization you do with your puppy should be in a controlled environment. You should never put your puppy in a situation where he has to defend himself from bossy or aggressive dogs.

Puppies need to socialize with other puppies and with dogs of all sizes.

Socialization outside the home

Socializing your puppy outside the home environment is very important. During the ages of eight to sixteen weeks, you should socialize your puppy to as many different situations as possible. If your puppy is small and easy to carry, you can start by carrying him to places that allow dogs, such as the bank, home improvement stores, pet stores, etc. During this time, allow people to pet the puppy while you are holding it. You can also go to dog-friendly restaurants or coffee shops, sit on the patio, and watch people walk by. Go to a local parking lot and sit with your puppy while cars go by. If you do not have children, you should find some and let the puppy socialize with them. The key is to get your puppy out as soon as possible in as many different scenarios as possible. Keep in mind to control these situations and not let the puppy develop bad habits such as jumping on people, barking, lunging, etc.

You also want to socialize your puppy to different people. Adults, children, old, young, black, white, thin, heavy, etc. Socialize to the mail carrier, the UPS driver, or any person in a uniform. If you are thinking of using your dog as a therapy dog later in life, be sure to socialize him around people with walkers, crutches, and wheelchairs.

You will want to socialize your puppy to different surfaces as well. Many dogs that have only walked on one type of surface, such as always on a sidewalk, will have difficulties later in life when walking on other types of surfaces such as dirt or sand. Have your puppy walk on grass, sidewalks, dirt, sand, and any other type of surface you come into contact with. You also want to socialize your puppy to different types of indoor surfaces such as carpet, tile, wood floor, etc.

Even though we tell people to socialize their puppies, many people do not understand what that means. They think if they take their puppy to the store with them on occasion, they have socialized it. Most people do not socialize their puppy often enough or in enough different situations. To make it easier, following is a list of things that service dogs are socialized to. Service dogs have to be solid in any situation. If you want your puppy to become an adult dog that is as solid and nonreactive as a service dog, we recommend you socialize him to as many of these situations as possible.

Surfaces: Dirt, grass, gravel, loose and packed sand, tile, concrete, granite/marble, slippery surfaces, puddles, water, fountains, carpet, and metal grates (where the dog can see through and may be fearful of falling).

Animals: Small animals, birds, cats, farm animals, cows, horses, reptiles, massive dogs, large dogs, and little dogs.

Equipment: Collar, leash, crate (wire, metal, plastic), harness, vest, boots, cooling coat, sweater, and basket muzzle.

Smells: Pizza, BBQ/grilling, food courts, exhaust (bus/truck/car), gas fumes, paint, rubbing alcohol, dog food (besides your own), something rotting, scents commonly encountered at job, and people who smoke cigarettes, cigars, and pipes.

Things: Bouncy houses/blow-up displays, full-wall mirrors, Nerf/water guns, vacuum, stairs, balloons, umbrellas, Hula-Hoops, PT/gym equipment, and soda/vending machines (money in, heavy thing falling).

People: Babies, toddlers, preteens, teens, young adults, men of all sizes, women of all sizes, people of all races, people wearing hats/coats/hoodies, police officers, EMTs, firefighters, people with an odd gait, people in a wheelchair, people with medical equipment, people with varying disabilities, people of varying ages, people with varying hair lengths, people with head scarves/face coverings, and people in costumes.

Events: Sporting events, birthday parties, holiday celebrations, church get-togethers, school events, seminars, street fairs, county fairs/rodeo, grooming, physical exams, and car rides.

Places: Dog shows, vet office, zoo, bowling alley, skating rink, movie theater, farms, woods, boats, and buses.

Sounds: Thunder, fireworks, gunshots, barking dogs, diesel engines, music, burning wood, crying babies, engines starting, hunting calls, and banging on pots or pans.

Car sickness

The car is another form of socialization you need to provide your puppy. During this time some puppies will have car sickness. The reason for this is because the ear structures used for balance aren't fully developed in puppies. They may drool, vomit or even defecate in the car. This is not uncommon and usually passes. There are different methods of socialization your puppy will experience during the whelping period with the breeder. Socialization to the car at this young age can help mitigate car sickness later.

In our experience we have witnessed breeders that never take their puppies in the car and breeders that take the puppies several places in the car. The puppy that does not experience riding in the car prior to his ride home is more likely to experience car sickness. In our experience that was the case. We adopted our Dalmatian Max at 12 weeks old from a breeder of a large commercial kennel that did not take the puppies in the car. He was fearful of the car and would defecate every time we put him in the car. Conversely, our bulldog Rudy was socialized in the car before we adopted him and he never experienced any form of car sickness. Rudy has always loved riding in the car and our dog Max also loved the car after months of training and many, many, messy rides.

You should take your puppy in the car frequently from day one, the younger your puppy, the better. You may have adopted an older puppy or a puppy that came with car sickness. In that case there are steps to follow to help correct this.

First and foremost, it is not the puppy's fault. Keep all associations with the car positive and do not scold the puppy for making a mess in the car. Any negative associations to the car will make it more difficult for your puppy to ever become comfortable in the car and will make the situation worse. If your puppy vomits, urinates, or defecates in the car, it is best to say nothing, just clean it up and move on.

 ALERT! Do not stop taking your puppy in the car because he gets car sick. The only way the puppy will get comfortable in the car is to socialize him to the experience. A puppy that never goes in the car will become an adult dog that becomes fearful of the car.
Do not take your dog in the car only to places that are less than pleasant, like the vet or the groomer. If your puppy has something unpleasant done to him every time he goes in the car, he will be less likely to ever get use to riding in the car. It is important to take your puppy in the car to places that are fun for him. I.e. the park, pet store, hiking etc.

To prevent making a mess in the car and for the safety of everyone, put your puppy in a crate. A crate is easier to clean than your autos carpet or upholstery. The crate creates a safe den like space which aids in calming your puppy. Provide a towel for your puppy to lie on to reduce slippage inside the crate and to aid in cleanup. Placing a chew bone or toy in the crate may also help distract the puppy but is optional.

Take a cleaning kit (a.k.a. diaper bag.) Keep plenty of paper towels, newspaper, wet wipes, water for cleaning, along with some bags for disposal and some deodorizing spray for the car. You will perfect the bag as you learn your puppy's needs. Be prepared to pull over at a moment's notice, to clean up the mess so your puppy is not sitting in filth and to insure that your puppy retains cleanly behaviors while in his crate.

If you know your puppy suffers from car sickness, there are steps to take to correct this undesirable condition. Allow your puppy plenty of time to digest his last meal prior to the exercise, the less food on board, the better. You will be using treats during this process so have your treat pouch handy.

With the car turned off and the crate in the car. Place the crate so that the door of the crate faces the door of the car. This allows you to place your puppy into the crate with both doors open, while you stand outside. Give your puppy some treats while the car remains still. Repeat this process for 2- 5 minutes several times a day. Keep it short and positive. This establishes a positive association with the car. Once your puppy is doing well with this, close the door, turn the engine on and repeat, without going anywhere.

Once the puppy is doing well with the car running and sitting in the crate, drive up and down your driveway or up and down the block. Repeat several times a day. Once your puppy is doing well, or having no sickness, increase the distance you drive to around the block, to the park, etc.

It is important to record the time from the beginning of the session to the point in time where your puppy becomes sick. (This will be referred to as his threshold.) For example, you start training at 10:00a.m. You make it around the block and your puppy becomes sick. Record the time he became sick, in this case 10:09 a.m. Your puppy's threshold is 9 minutes. Scale back the training session by a couple of minutes ending the session at 7 minutes the next time. Practice your training within the seven minutes not to exceed the 9 minute threshold. Once your puppy consistently travels 7 minutes without any accidents, then extend the session beyond the previously established threshold. Extend it to 9 minutes then 10 minutes, then 11 minutes etc. Eventually your puppy's threshold will extend indefinitely.

Some puppies will only suffer from car sickness a few times. Others however can suffer longer. If the first few car rides of your dog's life left him nauseated, he may have been conditioned to equate travel with vomiting. This is where the above exercises will recondition your dog by developing a positive association with the car. If the problem persists, you can contact your veterinarian for medication. The keys are to be patient, keep it positive and not give up. Happy trails!

You can see how much importance goes into socializing service dogs, and you should make it the same importance in your new puppy's life. The goal is to socialize him to as many of these situations as possible. You should always be on the lookout for new things to socialize your puppy to. We cannot say it enough, the more you socialize your puppy to all sorts of situations, the more stable adult dog you will have. Remember that all socialization should be kept positive and short, so as not to overwhelm or scare your puppy. Now, go socialize!

Chapter 7

Leash walking

A dog is one of the remaining reasons why some people can be persuaded to go for a walk. ~O. A. Battista

Proper leash walking is very important for a number of reasons. Most importantly, proper leash walking establishes the role of leader and follower for your dog, which is paramount for your relationship throughout his life.

Dogs have four legs and are meant to travel. Wild dog packs can travel twenty to thirty miles a day. Dogs need walks for their mental well-being. Dogs need to get out and socialize to become mentally stable. Many people say, "Our dog runs around our backyard for exercise so he doesn't need walks." Imagine if you were confined to your home and could only go out to your backyard. Imagine if you could double your legs (X4) and energy level (X2), and you could never go anywhere else—you did this for years, and there was never an end in sight. You would go stir crazy! This is what happens to your dog if you do not walk him. Dogs live in the moment. There is no tomorrow, there is no yesterday, there is only now. Many behavioral problems come from dogs that never get out of their home and backyard. The main excuse people give for not walking their dog is that they cannot control him on leash.

Proper leash walking allows you to walk your dog in a pleasant manner for both you and your dog. Dogs that are easy to walk are walked more often. We have all seen the people who walk with their dogs pulling them this way and that way. Dogs that are not properly trained to walk on a leash are not pleasant to walk. If your dog is unpleasant to walk, you will not do so, period.

We have also seen the people who walk with their dog on leash with the dog way ahead of them. When the dog stops, the people stop. When the dog pees, the people stop and wait. This form of walking puts your dog in the leadership role and is not proper leash walking. The dog will see you as the follower and that will lead to other leadership issues.

The benefit of starting leash walking with a puppy is that you do not have to break bad habits. You are starting with a clean slate and if done properly you will have a dog that never pulls on the leash, period.

Before going out in public and socializing with a leash, you need to practice leash walking at home several times a day using the praise and treat method mentioned in the previous chapter.

 NOTE: *Before starting any training session, be sure to allow your puppy ample time for elimination. If a puppy has to eliminate, it will distract him from the training process.*

Remember, the earlier you start proper leash walking, the more success you will have. No matter what the age of your new puppy, start NOW! The younger the puppy is, the stronger the natural instinct is to follow. Use this to your advantage! Remember the mantra, train early, train often.

Have your treat pouch handy and with a "loose" leash, start walking and get your pup's attention by saying his name. When he looks at you, say "good boy or girl" and give a treat. Every time—and we mean EVERY TIME—he looks up at you, say "good boy" and treat immediately. You will see that he will quickly learn that looking at you while walking on leash is a good thing. This will keep him focused on you instead of everything else in the surroundings.

If your puppy starts to get distracted and pull away from you, switch directions and call your puppy, using treats to lure him to you. You can also walk backward, patting your thigh, and saying your puppy's name in a happy voice. Most puppies respond to this and will follow readily. Do not go where your puppy pulls. If your puppy pulls, change direction or stop completely until your puppy returns to you and the leash becomes loose again. This will teach your puppy that he only moves forward if the leash is loose. Repeat this several times a day for five to ten minutes at a time. Remember puppies have short attention spans so you should keep the training sessions short and end on a positive note. The younger the puppy, the shorter the session should be. If you feel your puppy is getting distracted and not paying attention, you may have worked him too long. At this point, give your puppy a break and try again later.

NOTE: Puppies or any dog will reach a point where they "shut down." Which equals—overworked, underpaid, and exhausted. If you work your puppy too long, he WILL reach this point. The goal is to never work to the point of shutdown. If the puppy works to the point of shutdown too often, he will cease to work at all. You always want to end on a positive note and keep the training sessions short and rewarding to the puppy.

Practice leash walking in a controlled environment such as inside your home and in your yard. Once your puppy is following you 100 percent in these controlled environments, you are then ready to introduce distractions—e.g., front yard, neighborhood, etc. Once your puppy is paying attention to you on a loose leash in these minimally distracting areas, you are ready to go out in public. If you increase distractions and find your puppy not following, you may have increased distractions too soon. Go back to working in a less distracting area until you have 100 percent cooperation.

ALERT! Every time your puppy is on leash, he needs to follow you. If you teach him to follow you at home but allow him to pull you when you are in public, you are teaching him to pull when in public. Be consistent!

Once you are at the point where your puppy is following you in public, it is important not to let him rush up to people he sees and jump up on them. You should tell all people that come into contact with your puppy that he is in training and please do not distract him. If they want to help in the training process, they can be most helpful standing still and ignoring the puppy while you walk your puppy around them.

If the puppy is standing still and they want to pet him you can allow them to do so, but not if it makes the puppy jump up on them. If the puppy jumps on them, say "aghh, aghh," and use the leash to guide your puppy away from the people. Get your puppy's attention on you and treat when he does so. You can also step on the leash, which will correct your puppy if he tries to jump up. Any person you meet should be allowed to pet your puppy only if "all four are on the floor."

People love puppies and in a public situation, it is not uncommon for people to want to interact with your puppy and may even encourage him to jump up on them. If you allow this, you are teaching your puppy to jump on people when in public and are creating a situation that will be hard to fix once your puppy becomes an adult. Remember, "**It is easier to train good behaviors than undo bad ones!**" If this becomes a problem for you, it is useful to buy or make a vest that says, "Dog in training—please ignore." This is what many guide dog trainers use on their puppies during the socialization process. Most people will comply.

The key is to keep the puppy's focus on you. The puppy needs to realize that no matter what situation they are in, they need to look to you for guidance. You should also never put your puppy in a situation that is dangerous or in an environment that your puppy feels threatened by. As the leader, it is your responsibility to keep your puppy safe. This is how you build trust and respect from your puppy.

In conjunction with proper leash training, you will also be training other behaviors that you will use during your outings. These behaviors, which will be explained in detail in chapter eight are sit, stay, down, and most importantly, recall or the "come" command.

Walking your puppy should become a daily routine. Walking helps drain energy, reduce boredom, and cut down on behavioral issues. As your puppy becomes an adult, to keep his energy level low, walk him thirty minutes to two hours daily. The energy level of the individual dog will determine how long the walk should be. However, young puppies do not have the stamina of an adult dog; do not exercise too long. If you are a marathon runner, you do not want to take your puppy with you until he is older. According to the UK Kennel Club, puppies need five minutes of exercise per month of age up to twice a day. In other words, a three-month-old puppy will need fifteen minutes of exercise while a six-month-old will need thirty minutes. Once your puppy hits adolescence, you can step up the amount of time you exercise your dog. As mentioned in an earlier chapter, adolescence occurs at different times, depending on the size and breed of your dog. Smaller dogs reach adolescence around five to six months old while giant dogs reach it around eighteen months old.

While working with your puppy you have to take every situation seriously and use it as a training situation. DO NOT get lazy! If you are rushed or are not prepared to work with your puppy, then leave him home in his kennel. Remember that every situation is a learning situation to your puppy. Keep in mind our mantra, "It **is easier to train good behaviors than undo bad ones!**" You have to make time to work with your puppy and should create a schedule that allows you to do so. Many problems in dogs exist because the owners were not consistent with their puppy training. If you make your puppy mind at home but get lazy and let him pull on the leash and jump on people in public, you are in fact training your puppy to act this way in public. He learns two sets of rules, one for home, and one for public. What you do now in these formative months will determine what kind of adult dog you will have. Put the time in now and you will have a dog that is easy sailing later in life.

Chapter 8

Obedience

Properly trained, a man can be dog's best friend. ~Corey Ford

Obedience is important for many reasons. First, obedience builds a common language between you and your dog. As stated before, we are different species and in order to communicate we need to come up with a common language. Just as you have to teach language to a child, you have to teach language to your new puppy as well. Obedience creates that language. The only difference is when they go through adolescence; your puppy cannot talk back! Obedience also helps establish you as a leader. A dog that understands obedience commands is a more confident dog. Obedience builds trust and respect between you and your dog. Obedience helps control a dominant dog and creates confidence in an unsure dog. Obedience can also keep your dog out of dangerous situations. An obedient dog is more enjoyable in that he can join you on adventures outside of the home.

Obedience also teaches your puppy to "engage" with you, the handler. Engagement with you is the number one thing you want to teach your puppy. When in public it is very important for your puppy to be more engaged with you than with the public. By engaging with the handler, the puppy is looking to you for guidance and not distracted by the surroundings. This puts you in a leadership role. If the dog is not engaged with you, he will not listen to anything you say. He will not respond to his name and will not perform obedience commands for you when in a distracted situation. Lack of engagement equals lack of trust and respect to the handler. The number one commonality of all the dogs that come through our boarding school program is that they do not engage with the human at all. The first thing we teach in our boarding school is engagement. Until you have engagement, you cannot train further behaviors. When you teach your puppy to engage with you, he will continue to engage with you throughout his life.

Obedience for puppies should be used in conjunction with socialization and should begin early. Many years ago, people thought you should not train your puppy with obedience until it was at least six months old. This was because years ago trainers used only compulsion-based training, which could break a young puppy's spirit. Compulsion training is when the dog gets a negative response during or immediately after an unwanted behavior, generally with leash correction. Compulsion training does not use rewards for good behavior; it is all based on corrections. This kind of training is too harsh to put young puppies through, especially during the imprinting phase of development.

Today, with the introduction of positive treat-based methods, you can start training your puppy obedience commands at a very young age. We start training our puppies' obedience commands as early as eight weeks old. Now, because of a very short attention span, an eight-week-old puppy will not give you a twenty- or thirty-minute down/stay, but you can teach the commands "down" and "stay." Puppies are eager to learn and the younger you start them the better results you will have, as they become adults. By training early, adolescence will be less challenging as well. Even if you acquire a puppy at age six months or older, start where you are. All puppies benefit from obedience training. Our mantra for this is **"train early, train often."**

Another reason obedience is so important is that you can use it to control your dog in any situation. If you are eating, it allows you to put your dog in a down/stay away from the table. If you have guests over, it allows you to control your dog without him jumping up and running around crazily.

We have heard many people say that they took their puppy to obedience classes but it did not "stick." There are three reasons for this. First, they probably worked with their dog during class and did the homework for the six or so weeks that the class was scheduled for. After this time, many people do not work with their dog daily if at all. People assume that the six-week program is all their dog needs to learn how to be a "good" dog for the rest of its life. This thinking is comparable to saying that children only need to go through kindergarten. A dog's training goes on for its entire life. Basic obedience is to teach your puppy basic commands that you then use daily for their entire lives.

The second reason is that people are not consistent with the training. They may do obedience drills with their dog but do not control it in other situations such as in public, when guests come over etc. The puppy quickly learns the person is not consistent; he only has to do these obedience commands during the drills but at no other time. Obedience is not to be used just during obedience drills; it is to be used in every aspect of your dog's life: when you go to the park, to a friend's house, out for a walk in your neighborhood, or to the veterinarian. Anywhere you take your pet, obedience should come into play. That is how you get an obedient dog in any situation.

The third reason people say that obedience did not work for them is because they did not establish the leadership role from the beginning. The problems they are having are leadership or behavioral problems not obedience problems. Obedience classes do not solve behavioral problems and sadly people wait until they are having behavioral problems to start an obedience program. Obedience helps with leadership but alone does not establish leadership. The Puppy Montessori program is a leadership program. By putting the Puppy Montessori program in place, you have already started a leadership program with your puppy and are one-step ahead of the general dog-owning public.

Case Study:

A few years ago, we were on a camping trip. On this trip was a young veterinarian that had rescued a large dog that she brought with her. The dog was tied out on a corkscrew ground stake. On two occasions, the dog lunged and tried to bite a child and us. Upon bringing it to the woman's attention, she put her dog on leash and proceeded to do obedience drills to show "how obedient her dog was." The dog performed the drills as expected. Despite the dog understanding obedience, the owner clearly used obedience improperly. It was also clear that she did not establish a leadership program with the dog. The dog has an aggression problem that obedience can help if used in the right context. Most importantly, the owner needs to put a leadership plan in place in conjunction with obedience.

The proper way to handle this dog was to never put the dog in a scenario in which he could potentially harm someone or behave in an aggressive manner. You cannot correct a dog for bad behavior if he is tethered thirty feet away from you. The dog should have been tethered to the human. At times when this was not possible, he should have been kenneled. While on leash, the human could work on sit/stay and down/stay while the dog was tethered to her and around other people. She had the ability to reward good behavior and correct unwanted behavior as it happened. Instead, the dog learned nothing and just knew that after an outburst he had to do obedience drills.

When we talk about obedience for the pet dog, we are not talking about competition obedience. Competition obedience is a dog sport where a handler and dog team work through a series of structured exercises under the direction and scrutiny of a judge. If you aspire to enroll your dog in competitive obedience, then you will want to consult a trainer or join an obedience club that will teach you the proper training for competition. The Puppy Montessori obedience works with the same commands but is not geared toward competition. We are not concerned with how "perfect" the dog is at performing the commands but rather that the dog performs every time we ask, so that we can use these commands to control our dog in any situation.

Start all obedience in an area with minimal to no distractions, such as your living room or backyard. Once your puppy is performing all the commands well in an area with no distractions, you will then gradually add distractions (such as people) and will work in other situations, such as in your neighborhood or a quiet local park. Eventually you will work in a high-distraction environment, such as a parking lot or local pet store.

NOTE: *Remember to always increase distractions gradually. If you add distractions and your puppy cannot concentrate, then you advanced too quickly. Continue working in the lower-distraction environments and advance to more distractions slowly.*

All training is based on three things:

1) timing
2) consistency
3) motivation

In other words, every command needs a response within one second (timing), every command has a predictable response (consistency), and every command has an associated consequence (motivation).

Most importantly, every command is delivered only ONCE before proceeding with steps two and three.

 ALERT! **If, for any reason, you cannot provide consistent motivation in time (positive or negative), DO NOT GIVE A COMMAND. If you do, you are teaching your dog to ignore you, and that is a NO-NO.**

One of the most common mistakes made by pet owners is repeating a command. For instance, they tell their dog to sit. When the dog fails to sit, they repeat the command several times, "sit, sit, sit," before they actually assist with the sitting posture. Consequently, they are teaching the dog to ignore the first command; subsequently they fail to give motivation for performance of the desired behavior until the third time they say "sit." Eventually, the dog will learn that the command is "sit, sit, sit," resulting in the dog failing to respond to the initial command of "sit."

When, in fact, you are training your puppy any new command, it is best to refrain from all verbal cues or words until the dog is consistently performing the desired behavior. Only when the puppy is consistently performing the behavior such as "sit," do you then pair the verbal cue "sit."

Another common mistake we see is that people do not use the proper tone of voice when working with their puppy. Many people give a command and praise all with the same monotone voice. The puppy then has a hard time distinguishing the commands or praise from your regular words. Some people give a command as if asking the puppy a question such as "SIT? Down?" When giving a command, it should never be presented in the form of a question. It should be calm but assertive and a little louder than your regular speaking voice. When praising, your voice should be higher pitched and in a happy, comically charged tone. Sometimes the reason that a person is having difficulty getting a puppy to comply is simply because of the tone of voice. The puppy does not know he is receiving a command.

Some people give all commands and even praise in a loud, angry-sounding tone, similar to a drill sergeant. This tone often makes the puppy wary of the handler and may lead to noncompliance because of fear. If you are having difficulty with your puppy performing commands, keep tone in mind.

Learning stages

There are three stages to dog training that must happen to train your new puppy anything. You cannot progress to the next stage until you are confident the dog has gone through the previous stage. The three stages are:

1) the learning stage
2) the reinforcing stage
3) the proofing stage

The learning stage

The learning stage is simply when you are teaching your puppy what the words mean. We use all positive reinforcement (treats, praise, etc.) during this phase to teach the puppy what we are asking of him. There are no corrections in the learning stage, since your puppy does not know what any words mean at this point. Correcting the puppy for not performing would be confusing and detrimental to the learning process. When your puppy starts to perform the commands without assistance, you have completed the learning stage.

The reinforcing stage

The reinforcing stage is just that. You are reinforcing what your puppy has already learned by frequently practicing what your puppy already knows. During this stage, you can start using commands and mild corrections to reinforce negative behavior such as breaking command.

For instance, you give the "sit" command and your puppy sits. Before you release your puppy, he breaks command and stands up. You can then give a verbal correction such as (aghh, aghh) and a snap upward on the leash to disagree with the behavior. With puppies, this correction should not be forceful—just a tap to let the puppy know you disagree with the behavior. If you always give the verbal correction before the leash correction, eventually your puppy will comply with just the verbal correction.

 ALERT! If, at any time during this stage your puppy seems to be fearful, confused, or appears not to understand the correction, then you must go back to the learning phase and teach your puppy what the command means. Only when you are sure your puppy has learned what the command means do you then continue to the reinforcing stage.

The proofing stage

The *Merriam-Webster* definition of proofing is: "Something that induces certainty or establishes validity." The proofing stage of dog training is just that. During this stage, you will test that your pet understands the commands by having the dog perform with distractions. At first, you will add minimal distractions such as another person being present while you are performing obedience drills. Gradually you will increase the distractions by performing obedience in different areas; e.g., your backyard, or in different areas in the neighborhood that are more distracting for the puppy. You will continue the training in different situations so that your dog learns that you expect him to perform in any situation regardless of what is going on around you. During this stage you are tempting your dog in areas and situations where he most likely will try to break command. This gives you the opportunity to reward when he is obeying and correct when he is not.

This is how you teach your puppy that he has to obey no matter what the situation is. Again, if your puppy seems to be too distracted or seems confused or fearful, you may have progressed through the stages too quickly. You must return to the previous stage until you are sure your puppy is ready to advance.

Food motivation

We need to take this time to talk about another very important aspect of puppy training, and that is food motivation.

Some puppies are more food motivated than others. The term food motivation simply means how interested your puppy is in food or treats. Training a puppy is much easier when you have a food-motivated puppy. The more food motivated the puppy, generally the easier it is to train. If you have a puppy that is not food motivated, you can create food motivation.

When people come to us and say, "My puppy isn't very food motivated," it is usually because of one of several factors.

1) **The puppy is being overfed.** If your puppy is leaving food in the bowl, you are overfeeding. Cut back the amount of food in the bowl at each feeding until the puppy is eating it all. Actually, you should be feeding so the puppy eats all the food in the bowl and is looking for more. If your puppy is hungry, he will be more interested in rewards during training sessions. Since you will be rewarding the puppy frequently, we recommend cutting the food back considerably in the bowl. You may even have to use the puppy's food as the training reward and not feed in a bowl at all until you start to see food motivation kick in.

   One technique is to measure out the puppy's meals into sandwich bags. For example, if you plan to feed your puppy two cups of food per day, put one cup of food in two different sandwich bags. Keep one of those bags with you for hand feeding throughout the day. Split the other bag into two to three meals: one part for breakfast, one part for lunch, and one part for dinner. If your puppy is still leaving food in the bowl, adjust the portion of food down by 25 percent until you have reached a balance where the puppy is eating all the food in the bowl and all the food in your treat bag. As your puppy grows, you can adjust the volume but not the technique.

You need to be aware how much you are feeding, and make sure your puppy is getting enough nutrition. We recommend using a high-quality kibble designed for puppies. Your puppy should continue to gain weight and should not look too thin.

2) **The puppy does not like the treats you are feeding it.** A hungry dog will eat anything, but if your puppy is turning his nose up to the training treats, and you know he is hungry, it may be that something in the treat is unappetizing to him. Simply changing the treats you are using may be all you need to do.

3) **The puppy is nervous or stressed.** If you have a normally food-motivated puppy, and he takes treats readily when you are training at home but will not take treats when out in public, it may be that he is too nervous in that environment. We call this "shutting down." Dogs that are nervous will "shut down" and will not take treats. You may have increased distractions too quickly. Continue working in areas that the puppy takes treats, be patient, and gradually add distractions. Again, make sure your puppy is hungry. A hungry dog will take food in any scenario. Once you get the puppy to take treats in a distracted situation, he will generally continue to do so.

ALERT! Remember imprinting. In early puppy development, we want to keep all situations positive. Some puppies are more sensitive than others. Know your puppy and slow down if needed.

4) **The treat is not motivational enough for the environment you are in.** If your puppy works in an undistracted area for one type of reward but won't even look at you when there are other fun things around (leaves, bugs, sticks, flowers, etc.), the food is not a high enough valued reward for the puppy. You should have several different "values" of reward. For instance, when at home use your pet's food (low-value reward); when you are outside use cut-up food roll (medium-value reward). When you are in a higher distraction area, such as a park, you may have to use something more rewarding such as cut-up turkey hotdogs, cheese, chicken livers, or even pieces of cut-up steak. Try to keep treats natural. We do not recommend overly processed bag treats. Whatever

motivates your puppy in different areas is what you need to use. Experiment with your puppy until you find what motivates him the most in each situation.

- **Note**: *Some rewards are too high valued. In this case, your puppy will not perform any command; he is so interested in getting to the treat, he cannot focus on anything. This rarely happens, but if it occurs, change the treat to something less rewarding.*

   You also want to use a very high-value reward if you are asking your dog to do something exceptional. For instance, if your dog is chasing a bunny or bird, and you give the command to come, and he stops, turns, and comes, this is a time to give a jackpot of high-value rewards. For one thing, he deserves it for performing such a feat, and secondly, it will keep him interested in doing it the next time.

It is important to keep food motivation in mind when training your puppy. It is extremely important to have your treat pouch handy at all times, so you can reward your puppy immediately after he does something worth rewarding. Now, on to obedience!

The first and most important obedience command you will teach your puppy is the recall, or "come" command.

The recall (come command):

This command saves dogs lives! Having a dog that comes to you when called will allow you to keep your pet safe. For example, if your dog runs near the road and a car is coming, you can give the "come" command, keeping him from darting into the road. Once he comes to you, you can then put a leash on him. We have witnessed dogs having a rattlesnake drawn and quartered under a bush. A solid recall prevented these dogs from a potential snakebite.

The recall also allows you to stop your dog when misbehaving, such as barking at the fence. A dog with a good recall will stop barking and come running to you, when you give the command. If your puppy is off leash and gets something in his mouth that he should not, you can give the come command and he will drop what he is doing and come to you.

The first command we teach in the Puppy Montessori program is the recall. We will also show you how to teach the recall after your puppy is proficient at the sit/stay at a six-foot distance. Teaching the recall after the sit/stay is the natural progression of obedience and good for any puppy, especially if you acquired an older puppy (six months or older) that has not been taught the recall yet. First, however, we will teach the recall without the sit/stay command.

The recall is one command you should teach any puppy as soon as you bring it home. The younger your puppy, the easier this will be.

 NOTE: *To create a proficient recall, you MUST be consistent and you MUST keep it positive.*

The recall is one command that you will give "jackpot" treats for. A jackpot of treats means when your dog gets to you, say "good" and treat, treat, treat, treat, and treat. It is more rewarding for a dog to get a "jackpot" of small treats than to get one large treat. You should also make it a very happy thing for the dog to come to you by saying good dog and making a big fuss when he comes to you. If the puppy knows that great things happen when he comes to you, he will be more likely to come every time you call.

 ALERT! Never—and we mean never—call you dog to you to scold it. Never call your dog to you to do something that it does not necessarily like such as trimming nails, giving medication, or bathing.

As stated in earlier chapters, when you bring your new puppy home it will be either in the nursery or on a leash when out of the nursery. When you have your puppy on leash, get his attention by showing him a treat. Once he comes to you, say "come" and give a treat. Do this several times. Eventually, let the puppy wander away from you while still on leash. Once he is distracted or appears to not be paying attention to you, say his name and the word "come." When he comes to you, say "good" and treat. If your puppy does not come to you readily after giving the command, give a slight tug on the leash and show him that you have a treat. Once your puppy comes to you say "good" and treat. Most puppies catch on readily and will turn and come quickly once they figure out great things happen when they do. Perform this exercise several times throughout the day in as many different areas as possible.

The recall should be the one command you practice more than any other. The recall is also one command that dogs tend to ignore once they become an adolescent, especially if you have not properly established it from the beginning. The goal is to practice often, so it becomes habitual in your puppy before he becomes an adolescent.

As mentioned before, during early development, the puppy naturally follows you and will readily come. You want to take full advantage of this opportunity by reinforcing the behavior as early as possible.

The next command you will teach is sit.

Teaching your dog to sit and stay

Sit is a behavior that most owners want their pet to know and perform without any hesitation; sit is also helpful for teaching other desired behaviors like stay, come, down, etc. It is important to understand that there are several ways to influence your dog to sit.

Automatic behavior
We will start by describing how to reinforce the behaviors your dog exhibits naturally. Simply put, when you see your dog sitting (see Image 1), reinforce the behavior by saying, "Sit," and petting your dog (food treats can also be used to positively reinforce the behavior).

Image 1 - automatic sit

Assisting the behavior

For puppies, we use luring to teach "sit" (see Image 2). With your puppy on leash, show him a treat. With the leash in your left hand and the treat in your right hand, hold the treat over your puppy's head, moving your hand slowly back over the puppies ears. The puppy's head should follow the treat and eventually his butt should sit on the ground. As soon as his butt touches the ground, give the treat. Repeat this process several times WITHOUT saying the word sit.

Once the puppy is doing the behavior repeatedly without hesitation, THEN add the word "sit" as soon as his rump sits on the ground. After your puppy is sitting readily, you will test the training by saying the word "sit." If your puppy sits on command, he has learned what "sit" means.

If your puppy does not sit with the lure alone, you can lure the dog with a tasty treat, simultaneously pressing downward on its hindquarters. Remember that once your puppy is sitting, you have few seconds to give the verbal command "sit" and reward the behavior.

Image 2 - Luring to sit

Incorporating hand signals

Hand signals are important to use for a couple of reasons. 1) Dogs tend to respond more readily and quickly to hand signals than verbal cues. In our training programs, we use hand signals more than verbal signals to communicate with the dogs. 2) It allows you to give your dog a command when he is out of voice range but can still see you, such as behind a glass door or window or at a distance.

Once your dog is consistently sitting on verbal cue, you can incorporate a hand signal. Image 3 illustrates an example hand signal used for sit. While teaching the hand signal, it is important to remember your timing. Make sure that when the verbal cue is given, the hand signal is simultaneously presented. The hand signal for sit is taking your hand, palm down and turning to palm up.

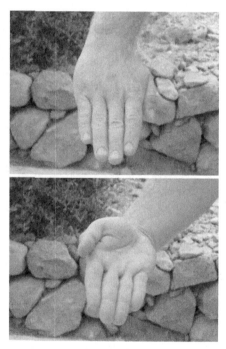

Image 3 - hand signal for sit

When teaching your dog to sit, the goal is for the dog to sit and stay until you release him. This is the goal with any obedience command you give to your dog. This is called behavioral integrity and must be taught. After all, in the long run, when we put our dog in a position, we want him to stay until we tell him not to.

At first, your puppy will sit, you will treat, and he will hop back up. The goal is to get him to sit for a period of time. Gradually over time, you will extend the length of time and distance for each behavior.

To create behavioral integrity, give your puppy the "sit" command. Once he sits, say "good" and give him a treat. At this point, you need many treats handy. As long as your puppy's rear is on the ground, treat, treat, and treat. You will see that your puppy will continue to sit as long as treats are flowing. After a few seconds of sitting, say "free" and use the leash to remove your puppy from sitting. Over time, you will continue to increase the length of time your puppy sits before giving the "free" command, and you will increase the length of time between treats. At first, you will treat frequently until you see your puppy holding the command for longer periods. You will see that once your puppy learns that "sitting" gets the reward, he will sit readily. Once he learns that you give a command to release him, he will sit until he hears the word "free."

If your puppy breaks command and gets up from the sitting position, and you are sure he knows what "sit" means, give a slight snap on the leash and say "aghh, aghh" or "no," and the puppy should sit. If he does not sit after the correction, you can hold the treat over his head again, causing him to sit. Do not repeat the command "sit." Once the puppy sits again, wait a few seconds and treat.

 NOTE: *Remember puppies have short attention spans so it is not reasonable to try to get a puppy to sit for twenty minutes at a time. Start with a few seconds at a time, increasing gradually to one minute, two minutes, etc. Practice all obedience in five- to ten-minute increments several times throughout the day. Keep it positive and always end on a positive note.*

Once your puppy understands what "sit" means, you will want to increase the distance between you and the puppy. This is when you will add the stay command (see Image 4 down/stay). With your puppy on leash you will begin directly in front of your puppy. As time goes on, you will say "stay" and take one-step backward so you are about a foot away from the puppy. You will do this until eventually you are at the end of your six-foot leash. If at any time, your puppy breaks command when you back up, step forward and say "aghh, aghh" or "no." Once the puppy sits again, wait a few seconds and treat. At this point, you can continue the session or, depending on how long you have been working, release your puppy and end the session. The goal is to achieve behavioral integrity; this takes time. Do not expect too much advancement from session to session. You must be patient because there is no shortcut for this process (behavioral integrity = patience + time).

Image 4 - down/stay

 NOTE: If the puppy seems to repeatedly break command when you get a certain distance away, you may have progressed too quickly. Start over from the distance where the puppy held the command. The goal is to eventually turn your back toward the puppy and walk away while he maintains the sit. This is the ultimate goal with any obedience command you give, and it takes time to develop.

Incorporating hand signals

We believe that when teaching "stay," it is important to incorporate a hand signal sooner than later. The hand signal we use for stay is an upright and flat palm (see Image 5).

Image 5 - hand signal for stay

Some trainers do not teach the "stay" command, stating that when you put your dog in a position he should stay without the added command. We believe that the stay command is an important one. There will be times when "stay" will be the primary command and will be used without another command.

For example, if you are walking out your front door, and you do not want your dog to follow, you can give the "stay" command to stop his progression toward the door. You may be carrying something such as groceries through your front door. Upon opening the door, you can give your dog the "stay" command so he will not approach the door. Many times your dog may be following you and you want him to stay while you continue walking but do not need him in a sit or down position. "Stay" simply means, stay in the position you are in and do not move farther.

Once your puppy is sitting in front of you and staying at a distance, you will give the recall, "come" command. Once your puppy gets to you, say "good" and treat, treat, treat. If you would like your puppy to sit once he comes to you, simply give your puppy the sit command along with the corresponding hand signal once he gets to you, then say "good" and treat. At this point, you can give your puppy the "free" command to release your puppy.

Incorporating hand signals
The hand signal for come is an upright flat palm facing you, extended away, and pulled toward you (see Images 7 and 8). For more timid puppies, you can also encourage your dog by patting your leg (see Image 9).

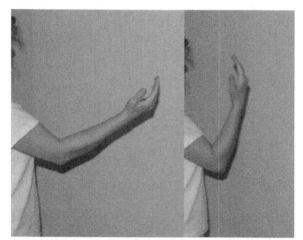
Image 7 - hand signal for recall

Image 8 - hand signal for recall

Image 9 - patting leg for recall

Teaching your dog the "down" command

The next command we will teach your puppy is the "down" command. We teach a dog to lie "down," or just "down," because it is the resting position and can be carried out for a long time. The extended duration of a "down" position from your dog is something that will take perfect practice and a considerable amount of patience to perfect. In our opinion, "down" is one of the most difficult behaviors for some puppies to carry out because of a dog's nature to be a self-serving opportunist and live in the moment. So to obey something as constraining as a "down, stay" command, you must realize that a dog needs to completely trust and respect the handler. This trust comes with consistent, well-timed motivational stimulation. As in all the above behaviors, give plenty of treats during the initial phase of training the "down" command.

Once your puppy learns this command and learns that it is a desired behavior, he will perform it readily.

Automatic behavior

We will start by describing how to reinforce the behaviors your dog exhibits naturally. Simply put, when you see your dog lying down (see Image 10), reinforce the behavior by saying, "Down," and giving a food reward.

Image 10 - rewarding automatic down

Assisting the behavior

We will assist the "down" command in a puppy by luring him into position (see Image 11) and breaking it down into small steps until we get the desired behavior. This command is introduced only once your puppy has a solid "sit." Start with your puppy on leash in the "sit" position. With treats in one hand, put your hand in front of the puppy's nose and move your hand down until you are touching the floor. The puppy's head should follow your hand. As soon as the puppy's head reaches the floor, say "good" and give a treat. Repeat this several times. You are teaching your puppy that moving his head toward the floor gets him treats.

Once your puppy is readily following your hand, move your hand down and forward so that your puppy has to stretch his neck a little to reach the treat without popping up out of the sit position. Gradually increase the distance away from the puppy. He will eventually have to stretch his neck and his front feet to reach the treat. As soon as he does this, say "good" and treat. Repeat several times.

Once your puppy is stretching readily to reach the treat you will then hold the treat so that your puppy has to stretch his entire body to reach the treat.

At this point, it should be uncomfortable to do so, and your puppy will automatically lie down. Say "good" and treat, treat, treat, treat as long as he stays in position. Repeat several times.

Once your puppy is going into position readily and ONLY when he is doing it readily will you start adding the word "down." After several sessions of luring and saying "down," you will test the training. Put your puppy in the sit position, then say "down." If your puppy goes into the down position, you know he understands what the term means. If he does not go into position, you need to continue luring and saying "down" once he is in position.

Image 11 - luring to down

Some puppies will learn this command quickly and others will take more time. Once they learn the "down" command, they will do it readily.

Many puppies will want to pop up from the sit position and walk to the treat, if your puppy does this, disagree with an "aghh, aghh," and make him go back into the sit position. Continue the above exercises from the beginning until your puppy goes into the down position.

Most puppies will learn the "down" command quickly with luring. However, if after several attempts, your puppy is still popping up from the sit, you can assist your puppy by sweeping his front feet with your hands.

With treats in one hand, lure the puppy until you have him stretching as far as he will without popping up from the sit. With your other hand, sweep his front feet with your hands, so he goes into the "down" position. As soon as he is in the down position, treat, treat, and treat. Do this several times until he begins lying down on his own.

As with the "sit" command, once your dog is going into the down position readily, you will reward frequently as long as he maintains the "down" position. After a few seconds, release your dog by saying "free." At first, you will release your puppy after just a few seconds, gradually lengthening the time he stays in the down position. If you allow your dog to break command without releasing him, you must disagree with an "aghh, aghh" or "no," and put him back into position.

In any obedience command, if you forget to release the dog, the dog will eventually break position. This will teach your dog that he can release himself whenever he wants. If you allow this to happen, it will be harder in the future to get your dog to stay in the desired position until YOU release him. Remember, the goal is to put your dog in a position until you tell him differently. Remember our motto: **"It is easier to train good behaviors than to undo bad ones."**

Incorporating hand signals
The hand signal for "down" is an extended arm with a downward-facing palm. When giving the command "down," lower the extended downward palm (see Image 12).

Image 12 - hand signal for down command

The release or "free" command

With all training, we teach a release word so your puppy learns when it is OK to break the position you put him in. In the Puppy Montessori program, we use the word "free." You can use any word you like. Whichever word you choose must be used consistently by anyone working with your puppy.

Teaching the release command

When your dog breaks a command, disagree by moving forward, saying "aghh, aghh," or "no," and put him back into position. This will teach your puppy that he cannot break command before the release word. Keep track of how many seconds or minutes he maintained the position before breaking command. You will want to release him a second or two before he would normally break so he learns what the "free" command means. Gradually you will extend the time before giving the "free" command.

With your puppy on leash, put your puppy in the sit or down position (whichever position you are sure the puppy understands). Treat your puppy every second or two while he maintains the position. After a few seconds, say "free," and use the leash to guide your puppy out of position. Repeat several times.

To test that your puppy understands what the word means, give the "free" command without guiding your puppy with the leash. If your puppy breaks command when you say the word "free," he understands what the word means.

Incorporating hand signals

The hand signal for the "free" command is both arms crossed in front of your body sweeping outward (see image 13).

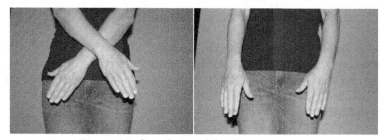

Image 13 - hand signal for free command

Use both verbal and hand signals simultaneously, and over time you'll be able to use either, depending on the environment. Once your puppy has learned all the commands, you can test your training by giving only verbal commands, and then only give hand signals. If your puppy responds to each by himself, he has learned what each means.

 ALERT! It is extremely important to make sure anyone working with the puppy uses the same verbal cues and the same hand signals for each behavior. If everyone uses different signals, your puppy will get confused and will be harder to train.

Keep all training sessions short, and always end on a positive note. In training our puppy, we want to set them up for success, not failure. If you ever feel yourself getting frustrated because your puppy is not performing, you may be moving ahead too quickly. Always take a step back and try again another time. The goal is to make the training process a fun experience for the puppy so he will want to perform for you.

Marker training

Many people over the years have asked us about clicker training. Clicker training is a method for training animals that uses positive reinforcement in conjunction with a clicker, or small mechanical noisemaker, to mark the behavior being reinforced. Clicker training was first used to train dolphins and has since come to include dog training. Clicker training works great for training tricks and is a great way to train behaviors. However, we have found that clicker training gets in the way of timing for most people. For the majority of people it is hard enough to manage the dog, the treats, and leash; adding a clicker tends to complicate the matter.

Clicker training is simply "marker training." The clicker is used to "mark" the behavior to allow for a longer span in time between the behavior and receiving a reward. For instance, you give your dog a command such as "sit." Once he sits, you "click" and then give a treat. This "click" tells the dog that what he did is correct and a treat is coming.

In this program we use marker training but with our voice. When your puppy has learned and is performing the behavior, you should always say "good" and then give a treat. The "good" is the marker for your puppy that he did the right thing and a treat is coming. You should use the term "good" every time your puppy does something you request, followed by a reward. It is important not to give the word while simultaneously giving the treat. Instead, say the word "good," wait a second or two, and then give the treat.

You will soon see that whenever you say the word "good" to your puppy, he will automatically look at you.

The benefit of using your voice over a clicker is that it is always with you, and everyone has one. Using your voice also reinforces the personal relationship with your dog. The principles are the same.

Chapter 9

Unwanted behaviors

Training a puppy is like raising a child. Every single interaction is a training opportunity. ~Ian Dunbar

Unwanted behaviors are no more than natural behaviors of a puppy that we humans see as destructive. Chewing, digging, jumping up, and barking are all natural behaviors for your puppy to engage in; that is why they do so. It is our responsibility to teach the puppy that these behaviors are undesirable and unwanted. The Puppy Montessori program does just that. If you follow this program to the letter, your puppy will not engage in these behaviors for very long if ever. Many people foster these behaviors unknowingly. Many of these behaviors are simply because the puppy was given too much freedom too soon. If you are using the puppy Montessori program correctly, your puppy will not be given such freedom until it is ready. Your puppy will be constantly supervised or will be in the nursery. The key to preventing any of these unwanted behaviors is to never let them happen in the first place. We understand, however, that many of you may have adopted a pet that already exhibits destructive behaviors, and you need to know how to eliminate them.

Behavioral extinction: We want to take this time to talk about behavioral extinction. Per Kendra Cherry, a psychology expert, in psychology, extinction refers to the gradual weakening of a conditioned response that results in the behavior decreasing or disappearing.

In classical conditioning, the conditioned response is the learned response to the previously neutral stimulus. For example, when you open a bag of treats in your kitchen, and your dog comes running to you at the sound of the bag opening, because you have fed him at that time. Your dog has been conditioned that the sound of the bag means treats are coming.

For example, your dog will beg at the table if he is fed from the table. You are basically rewarding the dog for begging and training him to beg. By feeding the dog when he sits by the table, you are reinforcing the behavior of "sitting at the table." If you stop feeding your dog from the table, he will eventually cease to beg because he is not getting a reward for begging. You have weakened the conditioned response of sitting at the table. You have made the behavior extinct by discontinuing the reward or reinforcer.

Extinction bursts

An extinction burst occurs when you first stop reinforcing your pet's behavior. Per Kendra Cherry, an extinction burst is "a sharp increase in the frequency of a behavior that is on extinction. Extinction bursts usually occur soon after a behavior is placed on extinction. It is a rapid burst of responses that occurs when extinction is first implemented." This simply means the behavior will get worse before it gets better.

For instance, if I gave you a $10 bill every time you clapped your hands, you would clap your hands. If I gave you a $10 bill only every fourth time you clapped your hands, you would clap until you received the reward. If I suddenly stop giving you any money for clapping your hands, you would start to clap more (especially if you were being reinforced only every fourth time), and you would probably clap louder to try to get the reward. You would even start to say, "Hey, I'm clapping—come on, give me the money." Eventually you would realize that no more money was coming, and you would stop clapping. That is an extinction burst.

During an extinction burst, it is very important not to reward the dog at all. For instance, If you have taught your dog to beg at the table by feeding him periodically while he sits there and suddenly you stop feeding him from the table, you may witness your pet performing a number of behaviors in succession:

1) He will move closer to you, making strong eye contact or (sad eyes).
2) He will make a sound—a whine or a whimper.
3) He will paw at you.
4) He will start barking loudly.

If you do not feed your puppy from the table, eventually he will learn that the reinforcer for sitting at the table is gone and will no longer sit at the table. If you feed him food from the table at any time during this extinction burst, you have just taught your dog that the current behavior gets the reward and that is exactly where he will begin the next time. From there, you will witness a rapid escalation. Therefore, the next time you sit at the table he will paw at you and bark loudly to get the reward instead of sitting quietly. You have just reinforced the behavior.

Case Study:

While at the vet with a puppy in training, I noticed an elderly man walk in with his small dog. The man had the dog on a leash and she was very reluctant to come into the office. He picked her up and carried her in. All the while she was clutching his neck with her paws trying to climb over his back. Once inside he placed her on the floor. He checked in at the counter and sat down with his dog next to him. He said to me "She hates coming here." The dog looked at him, whined, and dug at his leg repeatedly, all the while the man saying, "Stop, cut it out, why can't you be like that puppy?" She continued to try harder and harder, clawing at his legs, whining, barking, and even jumping up in his lap. The worse she got, the more he kept saying, "Stop that!" Finally, when she became so unbearable, he picked her up and held her, rewarding the behavior. He had clearly rewarded during an extinction burst in the past and was continuing to do so all the while saying, "I don't know why she acts like this." As long as he continues to pick her up and "reward" her for the behavior, she will continue the behavior.

Remember our motto: **It is easier to train good behaviors than undo bad ones.**

Had the man at the veterinarian taught his dog from the beginning to be calm at the vet's office by rewarding good behavior, such as sitting quietly, and never responded to the unwanted behavior, he would not have repeated the above scenario. Since he has rewarded during the extinction burst, undoing the behavior will be much harder.

An extinction burst does not mean that the dog forgets the behavior. Per Kendra Cherry, "In research on classical conditioning, Pavlov found that when extinction occurs, it does not mean that the subject returns to their unconditioned state. Allowing several hours or even days to elapse after a response has been extinguished can result in spontaneous recovery of the response.

"Spontaneous recovery demonstrates that extinction is not the same thing as unlearning. While the response might disappear, that does not mean that it has been forgotten or eliminated. This is why it is very important that once you are trying to eliminate a behavior, it is important to NEVER reward/acknowledge that behavior again."

Extinction happens when we cease to allow a behavior to continue. For instance if your dog rushes the door barking with territorial dominance, the longer you allow the behavior, the more reinforcing it becomes to the dog. If you stop allowing the dog to lunge at the door by never allowing him to get to the door, it will eventually become an extinct behavior. The key word here is NEVER. If you forget to keep your dog from the door and he gets to lunge and bark periodically, it will keep reinforcing the behavior.

Therefore, if your puppy exhibits unwanted behaviors, you must keep behavioral extinction in mind and make sure you do not reward an extinction burst. On the following pages, we will address some of these behaviors and what to do to extinguish them.

Rewarding undesired behaviors
We cannot talk about destructive or undesired behaviors without first talking about how people unknowingly reward these behaviors.

Many of the behaviors dogs engage in are because humans are rewarding them in some fashion. Many people think that an excited dog is a happy dog, when in fact an excited dog is excited because he is rewarded for being excited. For instance, when a dog is lying quietly, very few people reward a dog by petting or praising it. Most people ignore a dog when it is lying or sitting quietly. However, when a dog is running around, jumping, barking, etc., people tend to reward the behavior by talking to the dog, engaging with the dog in some way, or by playing with the dog. The dog learns that excited behavior gets attention, where relaxed, calm behavior does not. The dog will then engage in excited behavior more often to get the attention or reward.

There are several ways that people unknowingly reward undesired behaviors. For instance, a person comes home, and the dog is jumping up, barking, and running around in an excited manner. The person starts talking to the dog saying things such as "HI THERE! Who is a good dog? What a good boy," etc. Some people will even give the dog a treat at this time. This is rewarding the dog for the excited behavior. The dog will continue to engage in this behavior whenever you come home, or whenever someone comes to the door if you always reward him for doing so. Eventually the dog gets bigger, and it is no longer acceptable for him to jump on you when you come home in your work clothes. The appropriate thing to do is to ignore the dog until he calms down, then reward with petting, praise, or treats.

Another way people reward unwanted behavior is by holding or petting a dog while it is lunging, barking, or growling at someone. It is a natural thing for humans to try to calm the dog, but by petting a dog while it is in a nervous, anxious, dominant, or aggressive state, you are rewarding that state of mind. You are telling the dog it is OK to behave this way, and this is the behavior you want from him.

The key is to reward positive behaviors and ignore or disagree with negative behaviors. It is also very important to pay attention to what behaviors you may be unknowingly rewarding. We have seen many people who state they do not reward the unwanted behaviors of their dog, only to find upon evaluation that they do.

A reward does not mean that you are praising the behavior and outwardly saying to the dog, "Hey, keep doing that, good boy." A reward to a dog can be as simple as eye contact, petting, pushing away, or talking to the dog.

For instance, a dog is protective of his owner, and every time people approach the owner, the dog stares, growls, and tries to bite. As soon as the dog growls the owner says in a high-pitched voice, "Sshh, it's OK. He won't hurt you, relax," all the while petting the dog on the head. The owner thinks she is not rewarding the dog, only comforting him and telling him it is "OK." This will work with a human child because the child understands our language, but a dog does not. Now, did she say, "Good boy, keep growling, all right, yippee?" She may not have said those words verbally, but nonverbally the dog is being rewarded for the behavior by the petting and the talking. Remember Charlie Brown's teacher—to a dog the words are "wha wha wha wha wha." By her actions, the owner was unknowingly rewarding the dog even though she thought she was not.

If you reward your dog for being calm, you will get a calm dog. If you reward an excited dog, you will get an excited dog, and if you reward a bad dog, you will get a bad dog. So, begin by rewarding the behaviors you want.

Many unwanted behaviors can be abated simply by giving the dog something else to do before he engages in the undesirable behavior. This is why we teach obedience commands from an early age. A simple sit/stay or down/stay will teach your puppy desired behaviors before he engages in undesirable ones. For instance, to prevent begging at the table—first never feed from the table—give the down/stay command in an alternate place before you sit at the table. This should be a place you can readily see, and it should be comfortable for the puppy, such as on a mat or his bed. Periodically, get up from your chair and reward the puppy with a treat. If he breaks command, you simply put him back in position and continue to reward periodically. Soon your puppy will automatically go to his "place" when he sees you sit at the table.

Following are a list of unwanted behaviors and how to deal with them should they occur:

Mouthing and biting

Just like human babies, puppies start teething, which is uncomfortable. They will chew on things to alleviate the pain. They also explore with their mouths so it is normal for a puppy at this stage in life to put EVERYTHING in its mouth, including parts of you. Many puppies mouth hands because we move our hands. This movement creates play or prey drive in a puppy. This does not mean that your puppy is biting out of aggression or that it will become an aggressive adult. Chewing and mouthing are a natural way that puppies explore their world. Some puppies are more "mouthy" than others. What YOU do about it is the important thing.

Under no circumstances is it ever "OK" to play rough with your puppy and allow him to bite your hands. Many people make this mistake, thinking it is cute to play with their puppy with their hands. The reasons it is never acceptable to play with your puppy in this manner are as follows.

1) **It teaches the puppy that it is OK to put their teeth on people:** When you allow your puppy to bite and chew on your hands, he assumes he can bite and chew on everyone's hands. You are teaching your puppy that biting hands is a good thing, and this is how we play. Puppies do not have the mental capacity to realize that they are only supposed to chew on your hands and not that of other humans. You are sending mixed signals to your puppy when

you play with him one way and scold him for playing that way with someone else. This will teach the puppy that he cannot trust you.

2) **A puppy's teeth are sharp:** Maybe your skin can take those needlelike teeth chewing on them, but a small child or elderly person's skin cannot.

3) **What you teach your puppy to do now he will do as an adult:** Maybe it is cute to wrestle with your puppy when he is small, but depending on the breed, you do not want a seventy-pound dog chewing on you or your family and guests.

4) **Puppies chew on each other and play with each other to establish pack order:** If you allow your puppy to chew on you, and he gets the upper hand, he will eventually see himself as the leader, and he may try to dominate people with his mouth when he gets older.

5) **You may end up in a lawsuit:** Dogs' teeth combined with jaw strength can do some serious damage. If for some reason your puppy did not learn bite inhibition from the litter, it could easily tear skin enough to require stitches. If this happens to a visiting child to your home or an elderly person, you may see yourself in court and your dog destroyed.

So, what do you do when your puppy bites and mouths your hands? Anytime you are in contact with your puppy, you should have a toy or chew bone at an arm's reach. When your pup starts mouthing your hands, you should say no and give him the toy or chew. The puppy bites hands because they are moving, which is play/prey instinct. So get your pup's attention by moving the toy back and forth. Generally, most puppies will take the toy or bone. Some will continue to come back to your hands. If this continually occurs, you should make a loud sound such as "Ouch!" and stop playing with your puppy. Completely ignore him, turn away, walk away, or put him in his nursery (see the chapter on the nursery). Either way, play stops. He will start to understand that "when I bite hands, play stops, period."

Your puppy will continue to test this but if everyone remains consistent, he will quickly learn that you are not an approved chew toy and will stop mouthing.

Chewing

As mentioned before, puppies teethe just like human babies. Teething is painful, and chewing relieves the pain. Chewing also loosens baby teeth to make way for adult teeth. All puppies chew. You cannot and will not stop a puppy from chewing. The goal is to keep him from chewing on unapproved items.

If your puppy does not have approved chew toys and is left unsupervised, he will improvise. He WILL chew on the furniture, your shoes, baseboards, and any other hard surface he can find. This is why you can never, and we mean **never** leave your puppy unattended unless contained safely in the nursery or kennel. The number one reason puppies chew on furniture or shoes or baseboards is simply that they have unencumbered access to these items. If your puppy is chewing your things, go to the mirror and take a good long look at the person responsible. Do not blame the puppy.

People frequently ask us how to stop a puppy from chewing on their things. The answer is you never let him start. By following the Puppy Montessori program, your puppy will be tethered to you, or closely supervised when out of the nursery. If you cannot supervise the puppy, he will be in his kennel or nursery with approved chew toys available.

By supervising your puppy whenever he is out of his nursery you can correct him if he starts to chew on your table or chairs by saying "aghh, aghh" or "no" and guiding him away with the leash. You should then give him an approved chew toy. The chew toy should be hard, such as a beef shank bone or a Nyla bone. (Rawhide bones are not recommended.) It is a good idea to keep one or two of these items in your freezer and give it to your puppy whenever he is out of his nursery. You will find, if your puppy has something enticing to chew on, he will ignore your furniture. You should also provide these in his nursery and kennel.

By guiding your puppy away from the furniture, shoes, etc., you are teaching him that it is not acceptable to chew these items. You should never give your puppy shoes, socks, or any other personal item to use as a chew toy. Puppies cannot discern one shoe from another. If you allow them to chew on any shoes, they will chew on ALL shoes.

 Alert! It is important to catch your puppy in the act of chewing every time he tries. If you are not paying attention to the puppy and he chews a table or chair leg for any length of time, you have just reinforced the behavior, and he will do it again. Remember, "It is easier to train good behaviors than undo bad ones." You cannot discipline the behavior after the puppy has committed the act.

By following this program, most puppies learn quickly what is approved to chew on and what is not. Puppies that are never allowed to chew on furniture or personal items simply do not chew on furniture as adults. The key is to NEVER allow the behavior.

Jumping up

Many puppies jump up on people. The reason puppies do this is to get your attention. The reason they continue to do it is that they are rewarded for it. Generally, when a puppy jumps on people, they either reach down and pet the puppy, or (if it is a large puppy) try to push it away with their hands. Both of these responses are rewarding to puppies. When you push a puppy away, the puppy may see this as play, which causes the puppy to continue to jump, and he may even start mouthing your hands as well. Small dogs tend to jump on people more than large dogs simply because the humans allow it. After all, a small dog jumping on you is more accepted by people than a ninety-pound Labrador. Small dogs, however, can still injure small children or elderly people with their nails and should be taught not to jump up on people. Even though they are small, it still hurts when they jump up. We have had many bruises on our legs from little dogs that jump up on us.

You will see many owners yelling at their dogs to "get down," "don't jump," and many other words, and all the while their dog is jumping all over someone. The reason for this is simply that the dog does not know what the words mean. In fact, as you learned earlier, when you pair a word with an action that the dog is performing, the word becomes performance of that action. For instance, the dog jumps on someone, and the person pets the dog or tries to push it away. You say to "get down," or "no jump," but the dog continues to jump. You have just taught your dog that "get down" or "no jump" means jump up, because you coined the behavior (jumping up) with the word (no jump) and rewarded it with a pet on the head or push away.

Puppies will try to jump up on you and on other people. Teaching a puppy not to jump on people starts with teaching him not to jump on you and your family. Just like any behavior, you and your family must be consistent. If one person in the home allows the puppy to jump on them, the puppy will continue to jump on others as well.

So, how do you get a puppy to stop jumping? 1) **Do not** reward the behavior by giving attention or petting the puppy. It is important to enforce this with anyone who comes into contact with the puppy. 2) **ALWAYS** reward non jumping behavior. Many puppies jump up on people, because many people ignore a puppy when it is calm but give attention when it is doing something annoying. (Negative attention is still attention to a puppy.) If you reward your dog with petting or treats when he is engaging in productive behavior such as sitting or lying down, you are teaching your puppy that this is the behavior you desire. You will see that the puppy will sit or lie down more often than a puppy who never is rewarded for the behavior. 3) **BE CONSISTENT**. You and everyone that comes into contact with the puppy must be consistent. If you work on the behavior some of the time but get lazy and allow the puppy to jump other times, you are continuing to reinforce or are training the negative behavior. Your puppy will never learn not to jump up.

Teaching a puppy not to jump up

When you are standing and the puppy jumps on you, turn your back to him, do not make eye contact, or talk to him. Remember, he wants your attention, if jumping does the opposite then he will be less likely to jump. Most likely, the puppy will come around you to look at your face; he may try to jump again. If so, turn around again. If you have taught the sit command this is a good time to give the command. When the dog sits, pet him or give him a treat. When you stop petting the dog he may try to jump again. At this point, say "aghh, aghh" or "no." When he sits again, say "good dog" and treat or pet.

Remember anytime you give a command, the goal is for the puppy to stay in the position until you tell him not to. Once you give the "free" command, simply walk away from the puppy.

If at any time the puppy continues to jump up, repeat the above process. Once the puppy learns that sitting gets the attention or reward, and jumping up is ignored, he will start to sit every time he approaches you. Some puppies will learn this quickly and cease jumping up; others are more determined and will take a little longer. The key is to know what type of puppy you have and not to give up.

This may not work if you have a high-energy puppy, one that is very persistent in jumping or one that has been rewarded for jumping in the past. In this case, you should have your puppy on leash. Step on the leash at a length at which, if your puppy jumps up, the leash will correct him. When the puppy jumps, say "aghh, aghh" or "no." The leash will become tight and pull him back to the ground. Once his feet hit the ground, give the sit command. When the puppy sits, say "good dog" and treat or pet. Continue this as often as needed until the puppy understands.

If you are sitting and your puppy jumps on you, DO NOT engage with the puppy. Simply stand up and walk away. Do not say anything or give the puppy any attention in any way. If the behavior continues, you can use the above exercises in a sitting position.

Whenever you are with your puppy, you should reward him for "all four on the floor." If at any time, you approach your puppy to pet him, and he jumps on you, you should continue with the above procedure.

Once you notice your puppy is no longer jumping on you, you can begin socializing him to other people. Your puppy should be on leash. When you approach a person with your puppy, you should tell the puppy to sit, and then allow the person to pet the puppy. Any person you meet should be told that you are training your puppy and to ignore the puppy if he tries to jump up. It is your responsibility to set your puppy up for success. If you are around people who will not comply with your request, you should not allow the puppy to socialize with them at this time. Again, if a stranger rewards the puppy for jumping up by petting him, the puppy will continue to jump on strangers even if he does not jump on you. Everyone—and we mean EVERYONE—needs to be consistent.

Barking

"How do I get my dog to stop barking?" This is the most frequently asked question we get as trainers. First, let us look at why dogs bark. Dogs bark for several reasons. Barking is natural for dogs and is not considered undesirable to them. It is unreasonable to assume your dog will never bark. Barking is one way that dogs communicate. One reason for barking is to alert of a perceived threat, such as someone approaching your home, a snake in the yard, another dog approaching the yard, etc. Some dogs bark out of boredom, because they are not mentally and physically challenged on a daily basis. Some bark out of fear of certain objects, sounds, animals, etc. Some bark in play. Some dogs are bred for barking such as hound dogs and will bark more frequently than others will. (This is where breed selection comes in. KNOW YOUR BREED CHARACTERISTICS!)

Some dogs bark because the owner has rewarded them for barking. For instance, the dog brings you a toy. You do not throw it right away. The dog barks, and you throw it. Bingo! The dog just told you to throw the ball and you did. He will go there the next time and every time he wants to tell YOU to play with him.

Many dogs also bark because they do not sense a leader in the household. Obsessive barking generally occurs when there is no established leader of the pack. The underlying result is barking out of fear. The dog will feel less secure and will bark at everything. If your dog sees you as the leader of the pack, you can then control when and if your dog barks, and you will not have obsessive barking.

Therefore, you see, there is no one simple answer to the question, "How can I get my dog to stop barking?" You first have to determine WHY your dog is barking before you can control the barking. If you leave your dog in a backyard all day by himself, he will bark. He has to protect the territory, as there is no leader present, and he will bark at anything approaching. If your dog is not mentally and physically challenged with a daily walk and obedience, he will bark to release pent-up energy. If he is controlling you by barking, he will do it repeatedly. Pay attention to why he is barking, and you can control your response to the behavior and therefore control the behavior.

By using the puppy Montessori program, you are establishing yourself as the leader, and should not have problems with excessive barking. However, if you adopted a puppy that has barking issues, start by following this program. The nursery/kennel, the tethering, and the obedience will establish you as the leader. Once your pet views you as the leader, he may bark to alert if someone is at the door or the doorbell rings, but you can easily quiet him.

Running away /playing chase

Many owners have asked us what to do if their dog runs away from them. The answer is, "Do not chase them." If you chase after your puppy, he will run from you. The chase will become a game to your puppy. He will repeat it over and over, and you will lose every time. Again, this behavior is because of giving the puppy **"too much freedom too soon."** Many people have this problem because they never taught a solid recall to the puppy. The Puppy Montessori program prevents running away because your puppy is tethered to you or in the kennel. By using obedience and working with the recall daily from a very young age, your puppy will come to you every time you call him, because he knows good things happen when he comes to you. The recall is your best friend to avoid this problem from ever occurring. You should also always have a dragline or tether on your puppy, so if he attempts to bolt away from you, you can grab the line or step on it and bring him back to you.

If for some reason, you reach a point especially during adolescence, or if you have dropped the leash and your puppy decides he is going to ignore your recall and run the other way, DO NOT CHASE HIM! Call the puppy to you, if he does not come, start walking in the opposite direction, calling his name in a high-pitched voice. You can even start running in the opposite direction. Most puppies will turn to follow you. Once your puppy turns and starts to come toward you, start praising by saying, "Come on, good boy, let's go," etc., while running in the opposite direction. Once your puppy starts following in your direction, continue moving in that direction but slow down until the puppy catches up. Once your puppy catches you—praise, praise, praise. You have changed the game from you chasing the puppy to the puppy chasing you! Of course once you see that your puppy is trying to engage in the "chase" game, you should never set him up to do so again. You need to go back to tethering and working the recall.

 ALERT! Under no circumstances should you ever scold your puppy or hit your puppy for running away once he returns to you. By scolding or hitting a puppy or dog when it comes to you, you break the trust bond and teach him that coming to you is a bad thing. Your puppy will never come to you, and you will actually teach him to run away.

You may have adopted an older puppy that someone has done this to. If this is the case, your puppy should never be left where he can run from you. You will need to gain trust. Tether the puppy to you and work the recall repeatedly throughout the day, always keeping it positive. Someone may have tainted the word "come" in the past; you may have to change your recall word to something else such as "here."

Digging

Dogs dig for many reasons. Digging comes natural to dogs. Wild dogs dig frequently to find food such as bugs and rodents. Dogs dig to burry something they may wish to come back to later such as a bone. Wolves will bury the remains of a kill to come back to later. To wild dogs, digging can become a matter of life or death. Therefore, it is natural that your dog will like to dig. It is in their DNA.

Some dogs are more prone to dig because they were bred to do so such as the ratting breeds; Jack Russell, Dachshund, Rat terrier, Cairn terrier, etc. (know your breed). But in our experience, the most common reason dogs dig is out of boredom. Many dogs that are left in the yard for hours at a time have no way to release their energy; digging is a way to do that. If you leave your puppy unattended in the yard all day long, he WILL dig in your yard. Not only will your puppy dig in your flowerbeds, he will also dig up your irrigation system, pool plumbing, garden and more if left to his own devices. So, in reading this book to this point, what do you think our answer would be to the question, "How do I get my dog to stop digging"? **Do not leave your puppy unattended in the yard...period, ever...**

 ALERT! One reason dogs dig up irrigation and pool pipes is that they hear the water moving through the pipes and think it is an animal, which brings out the prey drive. If you have irrigation in your backyard, it is imperative not to leave your puppy alone in the backyard.

If you have a flower or vegetable garden, it is not acceptable to think your puppy will never dig in these areas. Your puppy sees you digging in these areas. The soil is soft and easy to dig, and in the case of a vegetable garden, there is food! If you have a garden, you need to construct a fence so that your puppy cannot get to these areas. If you allow your puppy to get to these areas, he will help you garden! (Results may vary.) The best way to keep your puppy from digging in the garden is to NEVER allow him to do so. If he is never allowed to dig in the garden as a puppy, he will cease to do so.

If you are outside with your puppy and you see him start to dig in an unapproved area, we recommend using a loud noise such as a whistle and a marker to disagree with the behavior such as "no" or "aghh, aghh," and redirect him with a more appropriate thing to do such as play fetch.

You have to catch your dog digging to stop the digging. If you leave your puppy unattended, you cannot do that. Remember, the Puppy Montessori program is all about being a "responsible" puppy owner. Responsible puppy owners DO NOT leave their puppy alone in the backyard for the entire day.

If you do have a digging breed and just cannot control the digging, you can provide them with a place to dig. You can construct a digging box or area that is approved to dig in. You can make a child's sandbox or just an area in your yard with loose soil for your pet to dig in. Bury your pet's toys, bones, and even treats in this area and encourage him to dig there. Most dogs will dig in this area if it is enticing enough.

As trainers, these are the most destructive behaviors we are asked about. There are other behaviors that will be individual to each dog and each living situation. Many destructive behaviors surface because of humans giving the puppy too much freedom too soon, lack of structure, or by well-meaning people who just fail to "disagree" with the behaviors and allow them to continue. Remember our mantra: **"It is easier to train good behaviors than to undo bad ones!"** Just like children who will get into trouble if not kept busy with structured activities, puppies will do the same.

If you focus on training good behaviors, you will see that your puppy will be so busy performing those behaviors that he ceases to ever engage in the bad ones.

Chapter 10

Health and Vaccinations

Whoever said you can't buy happiness forgot little puppies. ~Gene Hill

No matter where you acquire your puppy, you will want to schedule a visit to the veterinarian as soon as possible. Many people think that because the puppy received its first vaccinations by the breeder or the shelter that they do not need to see a vet until the next vaccinations are due. This is not true. Even if your puppy got its first set of vaccinations before you acquired it, you will still want to see your own veterinarian to have a thorough health evaluation. Your veterinarian will not only give you a vaccination schedule but also will listen to your puppy's heart, lungs, and abdomen, check for ear infections, upper respiratory infections, and check for worms or parasites. We have seen puppies that come with ear infections, worms, or even canine cough. Even if you think your puppy is healthy, it is wise to have a check from a veterinarian.

Another reason for taking your new puppy to the veterinarian as soon as possible is to socialize your puppy to the process from a young age. If the puppy goes to the vet and nothing bad happens, he will be more likely to enjoy going to the vet in the future. Whenever you are socializing your pet, you should include your vet's office as part of the socialization process. Let the staff handle the puppy, play with the puppy, give him treats, and even weigh him. If you do this on a weekly basis, you will have a puppy and later an adult dog that actually enjoys going to the vet.

Just as children have a set number of immunizations they need to stay healthy, so do puppies. Vaccinations are the most important thing you can do for the health of your pet. There are several core vaccinations that all puppies are required to have. These typically include distemper, parvo, hepatitis, parainfluenza, and rabies. There are also noncore vaccinations that include corona, bordetella, and leptospirosis. Veterinarians give core vaccinations regardless of what part of the country you live in. Your vet may give noncore vaccinations based on the area of country you live or certain situations, such as bordetella (canine cough) if you plan to board your dog or send it to day care.

Following is a list of diseases your puppy should be vaccinated for, which vaccines cover these diseases, and the order they should be given. This is intended to be a summary. For more detailed information, you can visit the sources listed in appendix A.

- **Canine Distemper**—Canine distemper is a virus that affects a dog's respiratory, gastrointestinal, and central nervous systems, as well as the conjunctival membranes of the eye. The first signs of canine distemper include sneezing, coughing, and thick mucus coming from the eyes and nose. Fever, lethargy, sudden vomiting and diarrhea, depression, and loss of appetite are also symptoms of the virus.

  The virus is passed from dog to dog through direct contact with fresh urine, blood, or saliva. Sneezing, coughing, and sharing food and water bowls are all possible ways for the virus to be passed on. Unvaccinated puppies and adolescent dogs are most vulnerable to the distemper virus. They are typically rescues with unknown vaccination histories, or they have been bought from pet stores. Serious infections are most often seen in puppies or adolescent dogs. Puppies younger than seven weeks, born to mothers who have not been vaccinated against the virus, are extremely susceptible. Once infected, puppies are severely weakened. Often the virus travels to the brain, causing seizures, shaking, and trembling. A weakened immune system leaves an infected dog open to secondary infections like pneumonia and eventually death.

- **Parvovirus**—The canine parvovirus (CPV) infection is a highly contagious viral illness that affects dogs. The virus manifests itself in two different forms. The more common form is the intestinal form, which is characterized by vomiting, bloody diarrhea, weight loss, and lack of appetite (anorexia). The less common form is the cardiac form, which attacks the heart muscles of very young puppies, often leading to death. Most cases involve puppies that are between six weeks and six months old. The incidence of canine parvovirus infections has been reduced radically by early vaccination in young puppies.

  The major symptoms associated with the intestinal form of a canine parvovirus infection include severe bloody diarrhea, lethargy, anorexia, fever, vomiting, and severe weight loss. The intestinal form of CPV affects the body's ability to absorb nutrients, and an affected animal will quickly become dehydrated and weak from lack of protein and fluid absorption. The wet tissue of the mouth and eyes may become noticeably red, and the heart may beat too rapidly. When your veterinarian palpates (examine by touch) your dog's abdominal area, your dog may respond with pain or discomfort. Dogs that have contracted CPV may also have a low body temperature (hypothermia) rather than a fever.

- **Canine Hepatitis**—Canine hepatitis develops as the result of infection by the canine adenovirus type 1. Similarly, there is a canine adenovirus type 2; however, this usually only produces cough, whereas the type 1 infection causes infectious canine hepatitis. The onset of the canine hepatitis vaccine has definitely reduced the occurrence of the disease, but it is still common in dogs. Because the condition is fatal, and there is no treatment option other than intravenous fluids for comfort and support. All dog owners should have their dogs vaccinated against canine hepatitis.

  The canine adenovirus type 1 is a rapidly progressing virus that usually begins by affecting minor structures of the body, such as the throat. However, as the virus progresses, it often leads to pneumonia once it has invaded the respiratory system. As the virus continues to spread and usually sets up in either the kidneys or the liver, causing one or both of these organs to fail. As the liver and kidneys begin failing, a dog may start having seizures, an increased thirst, and may vomit, bringing the dog closer to death, as there is no way to stop the infection. The severity of canine hepatitis cannot be underestimated. While the symptoms may appear rather quickly, the disease progresses even quicker, sometimes resulting in death in as little as two hours after the onset of symptoms are noticed. Even with all the modern technological advances in veterinary medicine, there is still no treatment method that can eliminate the canine adenovirus from the body, which is why vaccination is so important.

- **Rabies**—Rabies is a severe, and often fatal, viral polioencephalitis that specifically affects the gray matter of the dog's brain and its central nervous system (CNS). The primary way the rabies virus is transmitted to dogs in the United States is through a bite from a disease carrier: foxes, raccoons, skunks, and bats. Infectious virus particles are retained in a rabid animal's salivary glands to better disseminate the virus through their saliva.

  Once the virus enters the dog's body, it replicates in the cells of the muscles, and then spreads to the closest *nerve* fibers, including all peripheral, sensory, and motor nerves, traveling from there to the CNS via fluid within the nerves. The virus can take up to a month to develop, but once the symptoms have begun, the virus progresses rapidly. This inflammatory infection also has zoonotic characteristics and can therefore be transmitted to humans.

  There are two forms of rabies: paralytic and furious. In the early symptom (prodomal) stage of rabies infection, the dog will show only mild signs of CNS abnormalities. This stage will last from one to three days. Most dogs will then progress to either the furious stage, the paralytic stage, or a combination of the two, while others succumb to the infection without displaying any major symptoms. Furious rabies is characterized by extreme behavioral changes, including overt aggression and attack behavior. Paralytic rabies, also referred to as dumb rabies, is characterized by weakness and loss of coordination, followed by paralysis.

This is a fast-moving virus. If it is not treated soon after the symptoms have begun, the *prognosis* is poor. Therefore, if your dog has been in a fight with another animal, or has been bitten or scratched by another animal, or if you have any reason to suspect that your pet has come into contact with a rabid animal (even if your pet has been vaccinated against the virus), you must take your dog to a veterinarian for preventive care immediately.

- **Parainfluenza**—Canine parainfluenza is a highly contagious respiratory disease that is frequently confused with kennel cough. While the symptoms are very similar, canine parainfluenza is actually a major factor that can cause kennel cough, which is an acute inflammation of the upper airways. The disease can progress to pneumonia in puppies or chronic bronchitis in older dogs. The canine parainfluenza virus is transmitted through contact with the nasal secretions of dogs that are infected with the disease. Because the virus spreads fast among dogs housed in kennels or those that visit veterinary clinics, it is very important to choose reputable facilities. Do not take your dog to a kennel that does not require proof of vaccinations. You are asking for trouble!

There are a few factors that can heighten the chance of a dog contacting the canine parainfluenza virus. High humidity and exposure to drafts can enhance a dog's susceptibility to the disease. An unproductive, but persistent cough is one of the common symptoms of canine parainfluenza. The cough generally lasts ten to twenty-one days. Activity or excitement can intensify the condition. Dogs with canine parainfluenza have a runny nasal discharge. It is what people often refer to as a "snotty nose." Canine parainfluenza can cause a dog to have trouble breathing. The labored breathing becomes more acute with physical activity and excitement. Dogs suffering from the parainfluenza virus will appear listless and lethargic. In some cases, a low-grade fever may be present. Alone, the canine parainfluenza virus is usually not a serious problem. However, when it teams up with other pathogens, it can turn into a serious case of kennel cough. In many ways, the parainfluenza virus seems to intensify the symptoms of kennel cough.

- **Leptospirosis**—Leptospirosis is a bacterial disease that can affect many animals. It is rare in cats, but more common in dogs. Leptospirosis is a zoonotic disease, meaning it can be passed from animals to humans. Leptospirosis is caused by a complex group of closely related bacteria of the genus *Leptospira*. There are several strains that occur in different locations and tend to affect certain species more than others. *Leptospira* bacteria survive especially well in warm, humid areas, and are often found in stagnant water (e.g., ponds). Wild animals can carry *Leptospira*. Therefore, dogs with a higher potential for exposure to contaminated water and wild animals and their urine are at a greater risk (e.g., living in rural areas, hunting dogs). Adult dogs, males, and large breed dogs appear to have a higher rate of infection. However, *any* dog can be exposed, since urban wildlife such as rodents may carry the bacteria. Most infections happen in the summer and early fall, and outbreaks sometimes follow flooding.

  Leptospira bacteria are shed in the urine of infected animals, though they can be found in other body fluids and tissues. Dogs can become infected by exposure to contaminated water (through both ingestion or contact with mucous membranes or broken skin), exposure to urine from an infected animal (e.g., contaminated food, bedding, soil), bite wounds, and ingestion of tissues from infected animals.

  Once *Leptospira* bacteria get into the body, they spread to many types of tissues. The immune system may clear the bacteria from most of the body, but the bacteria may "hide out" in the kidneys, and the bacteria can be shed in the urine for many months after infection. Treatment with antibiotics may help prevent long-term shedding in the urine. The severity of symptoms varies, and depends on the dog (age, immune response, vaccination status), the strain of *Leptospira*, and other factors. Some dogs may have mild symptoms or no symptoms at all, but severe cases can be fatal. Signs and symptoms may include: fever, joint or muscle pain—this may manifest as a reluctance to move, decreased appetite, weakness, vomiting and diarrhea, discharge from nose and eyes, frequent urination—may be followed by lack of urination, yellowing of the gums, membranes around the eyes, and skin (jaundice).

- **Bordetella (Canine Cough)**—Kennel cough, the common name that is given to infectious canine tracheobronchitis, is a very highly contagious respiratory disease among dogs. As the name of the disease suggests, it is typified by inflammation of the *trachea* and bronchi. This disease is found throughout the world and is known to infect a very high percentage of dogs at least once during their lifetime. It is also medically referred to as tracheobronchitis and *Bordetella*. Young puppies can suffer the most severe complications that can result from this disease, since they have an underdeveloped immune system that is still strengthening. Also at increased risk are older dogs, which have decreased immune capabilities, and pregnant bitches, which also have lowered immunity to infections.

  Symptoms include: A dry, hacking cough is the most common symptom. Cough may sound like honking. Retching, watery nasal discharge. In mild cases, dogs would likely be active and eating normally. In severe cases, symptoms progress and can include pneumonia, *inappetence*, fever, *lethargy*, and even death. Unvaccinated puppies and young dogs, or immunocompromised dogs might experience the most severe symptoms of the disease.

  Canine cough is usually caused by exposing the pet to large number of dogs such as day care, boarding facilities, or dog parks. Many puppies that come from shelters and rescue facilities that house many dogs have or have had canine cough. Canine cough can occur anytime your puppy comes into contact with a large number of dogs.

- **Corona**—Corona virus in dogs affects the intestines and can cause intense diarrhea leading to dehydration. It is transmitted through contact with infected feces and can be passed from dog to dog when they are sniffing one another or playing. A dog infected with the disease will usually show symptoms within days, though it can also transmit the disease for months after symptoms have disappeared. Dogs with weakened immune systems, younger dogs, and unvaccinated dogs are particularly susceptible.

  Corona virus lives in the lining of your dog's intestines, so the main symptom is diarrhea. Unlike diarrhea because of the ingestion of some foreign object, diarrhea resulting from corona virus in dogs is foul smelling, watery, and yellow-orange in color. In some cases, the diarrhea might also contain blood, though this is usually a symptom of the similar, but more serious condition parvo. Corona virus usually appears within two to five days of exposure and lasts two to ten days. It can lead to intense dehydration, so be careful to monitor your dog's condition and ensure it gets enough fluids. Other possible symptoms of corona virus include loss of appetite, depression, nausea, and vomiting. It is also possible for your dog to have corona virus and not exhibit any symptoms.

These are the most frequent diseases that your vet may vaccinate for. There are other noncore vaccinations such as Lyme disease, canine influenza, and rattlesnake vaccine that your vet will decide to give if your pet is at risk for them based on your individual situation. Now let's look at the name of the vaccinations, what they protect against, and the schedule of vaccines needed for your new puppy.

Core Vaccinations	
6–8 weeks old	DHPP–(4 in 1) distemper, hepatitis, parainfluenza, and parvo In some parts of the country this will be a (5 in 1) vaccine and will include leptospirosis. This will be called DHLPP Check for intestinal worms and deworm as necessary. Start heartworm preventative
12 weeks old	2nd booster DHPP or DHLPP
16 weeks old	3rd booster DHPP or DHLPP rabies
Noncore Vaccines:	
6–8 weeks old	Corona
12 weeks old	Corona booster, Bordetella vaccine (kennel cough), lepto vaccine, Lyme vaccine, canine influenza vaccine (H3N8), rattlesnake vaccine
16 weeks	Corona booster, Bordetella booster, lepto booster, Lyme booster, canine influenza booster, rattlesnake booster

Once your puppy has received its initial boosters, you will then revaccinate at one year old. It is customary after one year old to vaccinate for rabies every three years and DHPP every year. However, recently some veterinarians are giving three-year DHPP as well. Bordetella is given every six months to one year and can be given as a nasal inhalant or a vaccination. Check with your veterinarian to find which vaccination schedule he or she prefers to use.

Internal and external parasites

Another reason for taking your puppy to the veterinarian as soon as possible is that depending on where you acquire your puppy, it may come with a number of different parasites. A parasite is an organism living in, with, or on another organism. Canine parasites include fleas, ticks, lice, intestinal worms, and heartworms." Again, this is intended to be a summary. For more detailed information see the resources listed in Appendix A.

Fleas

Fleas are wingless insects (one-sixteenth to one-eighth-inch [1.5 to 3.3 mm] long) that are agile, usually dark colored), with tubelike mouthparts adapted to feeding on the blood of their hosts. Their legs are long, the hind pair well adapted for jumping: a flea can jump vertically up to seven inches (18 cm) and horizontally up to thirteen inches (33 cm). Fleas go through four life cycle stages of egg, larva, pupa, and imago (adult). Adult fleas must feed on blood before they can become capable of reproduction.

The flea life cycle begins when the female lays after feeding. She lays her eggs in batches of up to twenty or so, usually on the host itself, which means that the eggs can easily roll onto the ground. Because of this, areas where the host rests and sleeps become one of the primary habitats of eggs and developing fleas. The eggs take around two days to two weeks to hatch. This is why, If you do not use products that kill all stages of the flea life cycle, you may have to retreat two weeks later. Different flea products focus on different flea life cycles, so check on the bottle to see which one you are purchasing.

Depending on what area of the country you live in, fleas may pose no problem at all or could be an ongoing problem. Fleas are found everywhere but primarily like warm, humid environments and cannot live in extreme temperatures. You will find more fleas in states such as Florida and Oklahoma than you will in states with more extreme temperatures such as Illinois, with its frigid winters, or Arizona, with high heat and low humidity.

If you find fleas on your pet, you need to get rid of them as quickly as possible. Not to mention how uncomfortable your pet will be from constant fleabites, Fleas left on your pet can cause hair loss, secondary infections, tapeworms, anemia, and even death. Fleas quickly inhabit their environment, and once your home becomes infested, it can become almost impossible to completely eliminate them.

There are different products for treating fleas on your pet and fleas in your environment. Generally when treating your environment, you need to remove all pets for a period of time. To rid fleas on your pet you can use flea shampoo, flea spray, or flea dip. There are also a number of products on the market such as "Front line" that you apply to your pet's back. These products are good to use to prevent fleas from developing on your pet after you have rid them of fleas. Flea collars do not generally work.

If you bring your new puppy home and find you have fleas, the first thing you should do is bathe your puppy in a shampoo that is safe for puppies. "Adams flea spray" is a flea spray that is safe for puppies and very effective at killing fleas on the spot. You can use it before or after the bath and daily if needed. Adams also makes a flea dip that is safe for puppies. Dip is a solution that you mix in a gallon of water and pour or sponge over your pet. Be sure to read and follow all instructions carefully. If you do not feel comfortable treating your pet for fleas, you should contact your veterinarian or local pet groomer to do so.

It is important to note that you need to treat the puppy and your home at the same time. As stated before, you may have to treat several weeks in succession to completely rid your environment of fleas. Again, if you are not comfortable treating your area for fleas, you can hire a professional to do so.

If you are unsure your puppy has fleas, turn him on his back, and look at his groin and armpits. Fleas like warm areas. If your puppy has fleas, you will see the actual bugs crawling around or may see "flea dirt" (feces). Flea dirt looks like black specks of dirt, when it comes into contact with water it will dissolve and turn reddish in color.

Ticks

Ticks are external parasites that feed on the blood of unlucky host animals such as our canine companions. Like mites and spiders, ticks are arachnids. The brown dog tick and the American dog tick, examples of ticks that commonly affect dogs, require three feedings to complete their life cycles. Ticks are most active from spring through fall and live in tall brush or grass, where they may attach to dogs playing on their turf. These parasites prefer to stay close to the head, neck, feet, and ear area. In severe infestations, however, they can be found anywhere on a dog's body.

Female ticks will engorge themselves, become much larger in size, and will turn colors from brown to yellow or gray. If you find a female tick on your puppy, look closely; many times, there are one or more small males attached around the female.

If your puppy has ticks, it is just as important to eliminate them as it is with fleas. Ticks spread many different diseases that often cause death. Many of these diseases can be transmitted to humans. The longer the tick is attached, the more likely it will spread disease if it is a carrier. So the sooner you remove the ticks the better for your dog. Dogs with many ticks will develop anemia that will lead to death.

If you find ticks on your puppy, simply swab the area with alcohol, using tweezers, grab the tick and gently pull it out. The tick head, or hypostome, is barbed, which by design prevents it from slipping out or the host from pulling it out. Many times, you will pull the tick and the head will remain in the puppy. Do not give this a lot of worry. Most of the time this will cause a slightly reddened bump and the pet's body will either push it out or dissolve it. Rarely will it cause an infection, but it is possible. Keep an eye on the area and take the pet to the vet if you think it is becoming infected. It is more risky to leave the tick attached and risk disease than to remove it and risk infection.

If you find that your new puppy has many ticks, you will need to use a flea and tick shampoo, spray, or dip. This will kill the ticks on contact, which will make them fall off the dog or make them easier to remove. Once you remove ticks from your dog, put them on a paper towel and seal them in a ziplock bag. If your pet starts exhibiting signs of disease, the vet can use these ticks to identify what disease the pet has. If you live in an area of the country where ticks are common, you will want to use a topical flea and tick repellent on your pet.

Many of the products on the market that kill fleas will also kill ticks and protect against future infestation. These topical treatments are especially recommended for those dogs that live in areas with high tick populations. Speak to your veterinarian to select the best product for your dog and situation. As with fleas, if you identify ticks on your puppy, you will need to treat the puppy and the environment at the same time.

Internal parasites

Dogs are victims of several internal parasites frequently referred to as worms. The most common are the roundworms, hookworms, whipworms, and tapeworms. Of these four, only two are commonly seen in the stool with the unaided eye: roundworms and tapeworms. Your veterinarian will want to take a stool sample to check for worm eggs under a microscope. Even if your puppy has been given wormer by a breeder or rescue group, you should still have your veterinarian check their stool.

Most worm infestations cause any or all these symptoms: diarrhea, perhaps with blood; weight loss; dry hair; general poor appearance and vomiting, perhaps with worms in the vomit. However, some infestations cause few or no symptoms; in fact, some worm eggs or larvae can be dormant in the dog's body and activated only in times of stress, or in the case of roundworms and hookworms, until the later stages of pregnancy when they activate and infest the soon-to-be-born puppies.

Roundworms
A large percentage of puppies are born with microscopically small roundworm larvae in their tissues. The larvae are introduced to the developing pup right in the mother's uterus via migration through the mother's tissues.

Roundworm larvae can also be transferred to the nursing pup or kitten from the mother's milk. The larvae make their way to the intestinal tract where they can grow up to five inches in length. They start shedding eggs and try desperately to keep house in the small intestine of the puppy.

The eggs that the adult worms pass in the stool can now reinfest the animal or other dogs and cats if somehow the egg-bearing stool is eaten. When the worm eggs hatch, larvae are released internally to migrate to the animal's lungs where the larvae (remember, the larvae are microscopic in size) are finally coughed up, swallowed, and finally grow up to adults in the small intestine.

Female roundworms can produce two hundred thousand eggs in just one day. These eggs are protected by a hard shell, which enables them to exist in soil for years. Puppies with active roundworms in the intestines often have a pot-bellied appearance and poor growth. The worms may be seen in vomit or stool. If not treated in time, a severe infestation can cause death by intestinal blockage.

Worming the mother has no effect on the encysted larvae in the body tissues and cannot prevent the worms from infecting the newborn. Almost all wormers work only on the adult parasites *in* the intestinal tract.

Hookworms
Hookworms are very small, thin worms that fasten to the wall of the small intestine and suck blood. Dogs get hookworms from larval migration in the uterus, from contact with the larvae in stool-contaminated soil, or from ingesting the eggs after birth. As with roundworms, the hookworm larvae can also be transferred to the nursing pup from the mother's milk.

A severe hookworm infestation can kill puppies, often making them severely anemic from the loss of blood to the hookworms' vampirelike activities! Chronic hookworm infestation is a common cause of illness in older dogs, often demonstrated as poor stamina, feed efficiency, and weight maintenance. Other signs include bloody diarrhea, weight loss, anemia, and progressive weakness. Diagnosis is made by examining the feces for eggs under a microscope.

Whipworms

Adult whipworms, although seldom seen in the stool, look like tiny pieces of thread, with one end enlarged. They live in the cecum, the first section of the dog's large intestine. Infestations are usually difficult to prove since the whipworms shed comparatively few eggs, so an examination of even several stool samples may not reveal the presence of whipworms.

If a dog is presented with chronic weight loss and passes stool that seems to have a covering of mucous (especially the last portion of stool the dog passes), and lives in a kennel situation or an area where whipworms are prevalent, the veterinarian may prescribe a whipworm medication based upon circumstantial evidence.

Although they seldom cause a dog's death, whipworms are a real nuisance for the dog and can be a problem for the veterinarian to diagnose.

Tapeworms

Tapeworms are transmitted to your puppy through ingesting a flea. (Another reason you should rid your pet of external parasites.) Fleas eat tapeworm eggs, then jump on your dog. Through licking and chewing to rid themselves of the itching fleas cause, dogs will swallow fleas. Once in the intestinal tract the flea dies and the tapeworm attaches itself to the dog's small intestine where it grows and continues to shed more eggs. Tapeworms may also be transmitted if your pet eats a rodent, bird, or rabbit that carries tapeworms.

Tapeworms can reach four to six inches in length within the intestine. Each tapeworm may have as many as ninety segments, though it is the last segments in the chain that are released from the worm that can be seen in the stool or under the pet's tail.

Many cases are diagnosed simply by seeing these tiny terminal segments attached to the pet's fur around the anus or under the tail; they even move around a bit shortly after they are passed and before they dry up and look like little grains of rice or confetti. These segments of the tapeworm contain the eggs.

The typical generic, over-the-counter wormers cannot kill tapeworms. See a veterinarian for treatment.

Heartworms

Heartworm is a parasitic worm that lives in the heart and pulmonary arteries of an infected animal. The worms travel through the bloodstream, harming arteries and vital organs as they go, ultimately completing their journey to the vessels of the lung and the heart chamber about six months after the initial infection. Several hundred worms can live in one dog for five to seven years. Heartworm disease is serious and can be fatal.

Mosquitoes transmit heartworms from animal to animal. The life cycle of the heartworm is complex. An animal must carry at least two heartworms (a male and a female) in order for female heartworms to reproduce. Females produce babies, called "microfilariae," which are shed into an animal's bloodstream but are not capable of directly causing heartworm without first passing through a mosquito. The microfilariae must be taken up by biting mosquitoes, and transform into infective larvae over a two-week period inside the insect. When the mosquito next bites a susceptible animal, the infective larvae enter the tissues and begin a migration into the blood vessels. Heartworms enter an animal's bloodstream as tiny, invisible larvae, but can reach lengths of more than twelve inches at maturity.

Symptoms of heartworm infestation can include labored breathing, coughing, vomiting, weight loss, listlessness, and fatigue after only moderate exercise. However, some dogs exhibit no symptoms at all until late stages of infection.

Your veterinarian will check your dog for heartworm through a blood test. If your puppy shows no signs of heartworm, you can start your pet on a monthly oral heartworm preventative.

Heartworms do not show up for six months after infection so your vet will wait to do a heartworm test on your puppy until it is at least six months old. You can start your puppy on heartworm preventative as early as eight weeks old.

Spaying and neutering

Spaying and neutering your puppy is another very important aspect of pet health and safety.

Spaying and neutering are surgical procedures that veterinarians perform to render dogs incapable of breeding by removing their reproductive organs. When a female dog is spayed (also called an ovariohysterectomy), the ovaries, fallopian tubes, and uterus are removed. Neutering commonly refers to the castration of males and the complete removal of their testicles.

Many people have come to us after acquiring a puppy and have said that they want to breed their puppy at least once. We do not recommend this for a few different reasons. The main reason is that there are millions of dogs being euthanized each year because of pet overpopulation. By breeding your new dog, you will be contributing to this cycle. Secondly, if you are not a "professional" breeder, who breeds dogs for the betterment of the breed, you will be breeding a dog of unknown health background and could be potentially breeding dogs with hidden genetic issues. Thirdly, dogs that are not spayed or neutered are at risk for health problems. Spayed dogs are less likely to develop breast cancer and will not be at risk for ovarian or uterine tumors. Neutered male dogs will not get testicular cancer and they will have a decreased chance of developing prostate enlargement. Lastly, unspayed and unneutered dogs can have a higher incidence of behavioral problems including aggression, roaming, and urine marking.

There are many myths associated with spaying and neutering your pet, and we have heard them all. Following is a list by the Humane Society of the United States.

MYTH: It is better to have one litter before spaying a female pet.

FACT: Every litter counts.

Medical evidence indicates just the opposite. In fact, the evidence shows that females spayed before their first heat are typically healthier. Many veterinarians now sterilize dogs and cats as young as eight weeks of age. Check with your veterinarian about the appropriate time for these procedures.

MYTH: I want my children to experience the miracle of birth.

FACT: the thousands of animals euthanized in animal shelters in communities all across the country quickly overshadow the miracle of birth. Teach children that all life is precious by spaying and neutering your pets.

MYTH: But my pet is a purebred.

FACT: So is at least one out of every four pets brought to animal shelters around the country. There are just too many dogs and cats—mixed breed and purebred. About half of all animals entering shelters are euthanized.

MYTH: I want my dog to be protective.

FACT: It is a dog's natural instinct to protect home and family. A dog's personality is formed more by genetics and environment than by sex hormones.

MYTH: I do not want my male dog or cat to feel like less of a male.

FACT: Pets do not have any concept of sexual identity or ego. Neutering will not change a pet's basic personality. He does not suffer any kind of emotional reaction or identity crisis when neutered.

MYTH: My pet will get fat and lazy.

FACT: The truth is that most pets get fat and lazy because their owners feed them too much and do not give them enough exercise.

MYTH: But my dog (or cat) is so special, I want a puppy (or kitten) just like her.

FACT: Your pet's puppies or kittens have an unlikely chance of being a carbon copy of your pet. Even professional breeders cannot make this guarantee. There are shelter pets waiting for homes that are just as cute, smart, sweet, and loving as your own.

MYTH: It is expensive to have my pet spayed or neutered.

FACT: Many low-cost options exist for spay/neuter services. Most regions of the United States have at least one spay/neuter clinic within driving distance that charge $100 or less for the procedure, and many veterinary clinics provide discounts through subsidized voucher programs. Low-cost spay/neuter is more and more widely available all the time. Start with the low cost spay/neuter finder from the Humane Society in Appendix A.

MYTH: I will find good homes for all the puppies and kittens.

FACT: You may find homes for your pet's puppies and kittens. However, you can only control what decisions you make with your own pet, not the decisions other people make with theirs. Your pet's puppies and kittens, or their puppies or kittens, could end up in an animal shelter, as one of the many homeless pets in every community competing for a home. Will they be one of the lucky ones? We also need to add, what if every person you adopt your puppies to lets their puppy have one litter as well, and so on and so on. You can see quickly how one litter of six to eight puppies can lead to hundreds or even thousands of puppies in a very short time.

When you look at the pros and cons, you can quickly see, there are many reasons you should spay or neuter your new puppy. When is the best age to spay or neuter? The ASPCA states that it is generally considered safe for puppies as young as eight weeks of age to be spayed or neutered. In animal shelters, surgery is often performed at this age so that puppies can be sterilized prior to adoption.

In an effort to avoid the start of urine marking in male dogs and eliminate the chance of pregnancy, it is advisable to schedule the surgery before your dog reaches six months of age. It is possible to spay a female dog while she is in heat, but not always recommended since she may be susceptible to increased blood loss. It is always good to speak with your veterinarian about the best time to spay or neuter your pet.

These are the major health concerns for puppies that are preventable with routine visits to the veterinarian. Puppies can also have other health issues pop up from time to time that may require veterinary attention, so establishing with a veterinarian early is very important to your new puppy's health. The basics for keeping your puppy healthy start with current vaccinations, checking for internal and external parasites, spaying or neutering and regular checkups by your veterinarian. If you follow these simple guidelines, you will have a healthy, happy puppy for years to come!

Chapter 11

Grooming

Anybody who doesn't know what soap tastes like never washed a dog.
~Franklin P. Jones

Regardless of the breed you have adopted, all dogs need some form of grooming. To maintain good health and coat, all dogs need to be brushed, bathed, and have their ears cleaned and nails trimmed. Ear infections are common in dogs and are very painful. If left untreated, ear infections can lead to deafness. Regular cleaning will help prevent this. Nails that become too long will deform the feet, make it hard for the dog to walk, and will curl around and embed in the skin, causing pain and infection.

Some breeds need more grooming than others and need to see a professional groomer every four to six weeks. It is a good idea to send your short-coated dog to the groomer regularly as well. Even though they do not need their fur trimmed, having a professional groomer clip the toenails, clean the ears, and bathe your short-coated dog is a good idea. Professional groomers have professional products and equipment that will help with your pet's skin and coat and even help with shedding. Many times a groomer will identify problems that you could be unaware of, such as ear infections, fleas or ticks, lumps, and skin problems.

People often ask, "At what age should we get our puppy groomed?" The answer is—as soon as possible. As soon as you bring your puppy home, no matter what the age, start now! The younger you can socialize your pet to the grooming process the better. If you have a puppy that will require regular grooming, call a groomer to make the first appointment as soon as possible. Many breeders socialize their puppies to the grooming process as early as four weeks old. It is never too early to start.

To make the process easier for both you and your puppy, you should handle your puppy's feet; look in the ears and in the mouth several times throughout the day. By doing this daily, you will get the puppy used to being handled in a way that he will be handled by a groomer or veterinarian. It will also make it much easier to care for your puppy should he need you to remove a thorn from his foot, bandage a cut pad, or medicate an infected ear. This will also enable you to examine your puppy throughout his life and identify any problems he may have. The younger the puppy, the easier this should be.

You should wait until your puppy is relaxed to examine him. You do not want to do this when your puppy is actively playing or in a high-energy mood. When your puppy is resting, gently lift each foot and say, "Show me your feet." Spread the pads apart to look in between the toes. Handle the nails as if you were clipping them. Start with one foot and go slowly until you have examined all four feet. Reward your puppy with a treat if he remains calm. Look in his ears and say, "Show me your ears," and put a finger in them as if you were cleaning them. Lift the lips, looking at the teeth and say, "Show me your teeth," and again, treat when your puppy allows you to do this.

If your puppy pulls back or tries to bite, you should remain calm, disagree by saying "aghh, aghh" or "no" and continue the exercise, rewarding him when he is calm and lets you continue. You may have to examine just one paw or one ear and gradually move to the others. Always stop the process when the puppy is relaxed and is allowing you to examine him. This will teach him that fighting gets him nowhere and relaxing gets him what he wants.

ALERT! It is important not to quit the examination process if your puppy tries to bite or pull away. If you do this, you are teaching the puppy that when he bites or pulls away, he gets you to leave him alone. It will be very hard for anyone to do anything to him in the future. If your puppy bites or pulls away, continue to hold the puppy gently until he stops, then continue the examination. You should also never be forceful with the puppy or make it a bad experience; this will make him fearful of any future handling.

At first, when examining your puppy, keep the intervals short and as uneventful as possible. Do not take too much time on any one area. Do not take so much time that the puppy becomes frustrated. Always end on a positive note.

If you have a puppy that will need professional grooming, there are a few things you will want to add to this examining process. You will want to start by placing your puppy on a table or flat surface off the floor. Examine the feet, ears, and teeth. You should brush and comb your puppy daily. If you have any type of grooming clippers at home, turn them on and let your puppy smell them and look at them, gradually start moving them around the body without actually clipping any fur. Repeat these exercises daily, and your groomer will thank you.

If you adopted a puppy that will have long fur that can get matted, you will need to brush and comb him daily. Yes, daily! There are no excuses. Think about it, you brush your own hair and your children's hair daily, and you only have hair on your head. Your puppy has fur over its entire body; if not brushed regularly, it will mat. Once a dog's fur is matted, it becomes uncomfortable, and if it becomes severe, the skin cannot breathe and moisture can be trapped under the fur, causing skin and health problems. Not to mention the fact that removing mats is painful. If you take your dog to the groomer and it is always matted, the grooming experience is always a negative one for your dog. If a dog is severely matted, most groomers will strip the coat to avoid a painful, negative experience for your dog.

If you brush and comb your puppy every day, the process should take no more than five to ten minutes. Again, you should start this the day you bring your puppy home. If you are unsure about how to properly brush and comb your puppy (there is a correct way), you should ask your groomer to show you. Most groomers will be happy to show you how to do this correctly, as it will save them time from taking mats out of your dog when it comes for grooming. After decades of grooming dogs, we have heard all the excuses possible as to why dogs come to us with matted coats. All of them false. The only reason a pet's fur becomes matted is that the owner does not brush it daily, period. You should treat your puppy's fur just as you would your own hair.

If you are a person who knows you will not brush your pet daily, you should adopt a short-coated breed. If you have adopted a long-coated breed, have the fur trimmed to a manageable length by a groomer every four to six weeks.

 NOTE: *Brushing the dog's coat is a bonding experience for you and the dog. If performed regularly and correctly, it should be a relaxing experience for both of you.*

If you choose to bathe your pet at home, you need to purchase a shampoo for dogs and one that is safe for puppies. Human shampoo is not an acceptable shampoo to bathe your dog with. Humans and dogs have a different pH level. If you bathe your dog regularly with human shampoo, it will cause dry skin and can cause itching. When you bathe, your dog at home, be careful not to get shampoo in the eyes or water in the ears and nose. Keep the bathing process as positive as possible and reward with a treat once you are done.

If you have a short-coated breed, it will also benefit from regular brushing. Short-coated breeds tend to shed considerably and regular brushing will minimize this. They will need their ears cleaned and nails trimmed monthly and will need to be bathed regularly. You can do this at home if you are comfortable doing so; if not, you should have a groomer or veterinarian trim the nails and clean the ears monthly.

ALERT! When clipping your puppy's nails, be aware of a vein that runs through the nail called the "quick." If you clip the nail down to the quick, the nail will bleed. This is also painful for the puppy. You should never intentionally clip your pet's nails past the quick. There are commercial clotting agents on the market such as Kwik Stop styptic powder that you apply if you accidently cut the quick. You can also use cornstarch. If you accidently cut the quick, put styptic powder or cornstarch on the nail and apply pressure for as long as needed to stop the bleeding. Again, if you are uncomfortable clipping your puppy's nails, have a veterinarian or groomer do it for you. A puppy that has had his nails quicked will be difficult in the future when having his nails trimmed.

Following is a brief breakdown of some breeds and the minimal grooming needs they will have. You may wish to do these tasks more frequently, depending on your living situation.

Smooth coated: Doberman, Boxer, Rhodesian ridgeback, Chihuahua, and some hounds. These dogs have a very short coat with minimal shedding—bathe monthly, check ears weekly, and clean ears as needed or monthly. Nails trimmed monthly.

Short coated: Labrador retriever, Rottweiler, Dalmatian, and pug. These dogs have a little longer fur than smooth-coated dogs and tend to shed more. Bathe monthly, brush daily or weekly, check ears weekly, and clean ears as needed or monthly. Nails trimmed monthly.

Double coated: Any of the husky breeds, the German shepherd, Sheltie, Pomeranian, and Chow. These dogs have a top coat and an undercoat. The bottom layer is soft, dense, and keeps the dog warm. The top layer is harsh and long to help water roll off the dog and not soak through the bottom coat. Typically these dogs shed their undercoat twice a year in the spring and fall, when they are said to be "blowing coat." They tend to shed little during the rest of the year, but when they "blow coat" they really "blow coat," which can be extremely messy. This undercoat needs to be brushed out using special tools. If left unattended, the undercoat can become matted. Double-coated breeds should not be shaved down, as this may lead to problems with the coat later. Most double-coated breeds will benefit from regular trips to the groomer (every six to eight weeks) to keep their coat healthy. They will also need to be bathed monthly, brushed daily, ears checked weekly and cleaned as needed or monthly, and nails trimmed monthly.

Curly coated: Poodle and any mixture of poodle, Bichon Frise and Portuguese water dog. These dogs do not shed and are considered "hypoallergenic" because of this. These breeds need to see a professional groomer for trimming every four to six weeks or more often. These breeds typically have fur in their ears that needs to be plucked monthly. The eyes should be wiped daily with a water-soaked cotton ball to prevent buildup of eye drainage. Ears should be cleaned and nails trimmed monthly as well, and they should be brushed and combed daily.

Wire coated: Cairn terrier, Westie, Scottish terrier. The coat on these breeds combines a short, soft undercoat with wiry guard hairs growing through it to create a harsh, wiry, and weatherproof jacket. These dogs tend to shed less but also "blow coat" twice a year. They should see a professional groomer every four to six weeks or more often. Eyes should be cleaned daily with a water-soaked cotton ball to prevent buildup of eye drainage. Ears should be cleaned and nails trimmed monthly, and they should be brushed and combed daily.

Long coat: Cocker spaniel, Golden retriever, Shih-Tzu, Yorkie, Lhasa apso. These dogs have a long, flowing coat that can be left natural or trimmed into a more manageable length. These dogs should see a professional groomer every four weeks or more frequently. Eyes should be cleaned daily with a water-soaked cotton ball to prevent buildup of eye drainage. Because of the long fur and heavy ears, these dogs are prone to ear infections so the ears should be checked and cleaned weekly. Trim nails monthly, and brush and comb the dog daily.

Of course, many mixed-breed dogs could fit into any of these categories. Knowing the coat type and how to manage it is half the battle. There are also different grooming requirements for the show dog than the pet dog of the same breed. The important thing is to acknowledge that your puppy will have grooming requirements that you need to meet to keep it healthy. The earlier you start the process, the happier both you and your puppy (and your groomer) will be.

Chapter 12

Nutrition

My dog is worried about the economy because Alpo is up to 99 cents a can. That's almost $7.00 in dog money. ~Joe Weinstein

There are many types of dog food on the market today. Supermarkets have an entire aisle dedicated to it and pet stores have many aisles dedicated to it. Commercial after commercial on television explains why you should choose "their" brand of dog food. Dog food comes in all different packaging and comes in dry kibble form, canned, and even raw food. It also comes in different grades, ranging from economy grade to premium and ultrapremium.

So, how do you pick a food to feed your puppy? First, you want to feed a food specialized or approved for puppies. Even a lower-grade puppy food is better than feeding your puppy adult dog food. Puppies are growing and have higher protein and calorie needs than adult dogs. If you have a large-breed puppy, you may want to feed a food designed for large-breed puppies. Large-breed puppy foods are designed for controlled growth and may be lower in calcium and phosphorus than other puppy foods. Excess levels of calcium and phosphorus can contribute to skeletal problems. Large-breed puppy food also may contain more fiber to add bulk to the diet without calories.

You want to feed the best food you can afford. The more premium foods are a bit more expensive than the economy grade foods but the nutrition is so much better. Do not be taken in by fancy advertising. We have seen many commercials touting how great a dog food is, when in fact, after looking at the ingredient list, it was quite the contrary. Many people buy dog food because it is sold at the veterinarian's office, even though it is loaded with fillers. When choosing a puppy food you **always** need to look at the ingredient list.

The first ingredient should be a protein (e.g., chicken, beef, fish, etc.). Corn and other grains are fillers and should not be the first ingredient. You should also avoid foods that say "meat, poultry, meat meal, etc." You need to know what kind of meat or poultry is in the food.

Dog food comes in several forms: canned, dry, and semimoist. There are classifications such as super premium, premium, regular, or economy. The higher-quality dog foods have three advantages: 1) They are more nutrient-dense, which means less food goes in and less waste comes out. 2) The nutrients are readily usable by the body. 3) The ingredients remain consistent.

To reduce manufacturing costs, some companies use a least-cost formula. The ingredients they use in their food can vary according to what is available for the lowest price, so the food you buy one month could be different from the food you buy the next month, even though the brand remains the same. Premium and ultrapremium foods can be somewhat higher in price, but the fixed formula remains the same from bag to bag.

Generally speaking, the more premium foods result in a healthier dog. There is a good method for grading dog foods. This method of determining the best dog food is based on allocating points for high-quality dog food ingredients, and deducting points for inferior ingredients/fillers/chemicals, etc. The resulting "score" for each dog food ranges from an A+ to an F.

This method of grading dog food was developed by Great Dane owner and rescue volunteer Sarah Irick. She uses a very detailed point system to determine the overall value and quality of an individual dog food. She is a civil/industrial engineer, not a veterinarian or animal nutritionist by education or employment. She does not work for a pet food manufacturer and has no affiliation with one. She does not officially support any one food.

This food grading system is specifically to help those who have trouble deciphering dog food labels and the many articles about what ingredients are.

To grade any dog food using Sarah's dog food comparison technique, you need to start with the list of ingredients (it is easy to find an ingredient list for any particular food on the manufacturer's website, or you can use the list on your dog food bag).

Start with a grade of one hundred points, then:

1. For every listing of "by-product," subtract ten points.
2. For every nonspecific animal source ("meat" or "poultry," meat, meal, or fat) reference, subtract ten points.
3. If the food contains BHA, BHT, or ethoxyquin, subtract ten points.
4. For every grain "mill run" or nonspecific grain source, subtract five points. If the same grain ingredient is used two or more times in the first five ingredients (e.g., "ground brown rice," "brewers' rice," and "rice flour" are all the same grain), subtract five points.
5. If the protein sources are not meat meal, and there are fewer than two meats in the top three ingredients, subtract three points.
6. If it contains any artificial colorants, subtract three points.
7. If it contains ground corn or whole grain corn, subtract three points.
8. If corn is listed in the top five ingredients, subtract two more points.
9. If the food contains any animal fat other than fish oil, subtract two points.
10. If lamb is the only animal protein source (unless your dog is allergic to other protein sources), subtract two points.
11. If it contains soy or soybeans, subtract two points.
12. If it contains wheat (unless you know your dog isn't allergic to wheat), subtract two points.
13. If it contains beef (unless you know your dog isn't allergic to beef), subtract one point.
14. If it contains salt, subtract one point.

Extra Credit:
- If any of the meat sources are organic, add five points.
- If the food is endorsed by any major breed group or nutritionist, add five points.
- If the food is baked not extruded, add five points.
- If the food contains probiotics, add three points.
- If the food contains fruit, add three points.
- If the food contains vegetables (NOT corn or other grains), add three points.
- If hormone-free and antibiotic-free animal sources are used, add two points.
- If the food contains barley, add two points.
- If the food contains flax seed oil (not just the seeds), add two points.
- If the food contains oats or oatmeal, add one point.
- If the food contains sunflower oil, add one point.
- For every different specific animal protein source (other than the first one; count "chicken" and "chicken meal" as only one protein source, but "chicken" and "fish" as two different sources), add one point.
- If it contains glucosamine and chondroitin, add one point.
- If pesticide-free vegetables are used, add one point.

SCORING
94-100+ = A
86-93 = B
78-85 = C
70-77 = D
<70 = F

For instance, dog foods such as Beneful, Bil•Jack Select, and Science Diet large breed have a score of F. Foods such as Alpo Prime Cuts, Eukanuba puppy and adult and Pronature puppy have a score of C. Foods such as Blue Buffalo chicken and rice, Natural Balance Ultra, and Kirkland Signature chicken, rice, and vegetables have a score of A+.

See appendix B for a more complete list of specific dog food brands and additional details. The point is, even if you cannot afford an ultrapremium food, it is better to feed your pet a food with a C rating rather than an F rating. The phrase "you are what you eat" applies to your puppy as well.

The next question new puppy owners have is "How much do I feed my puppy?" We will tell you right now that most people overfeed their dogs. The amounts on the dog food bag are always too much. After all, the more you feed the more dog food you must buy.

Much depends on the size of puppy you have. Obviously, you will feed a Great Dane puppy more than a Chihuahua puppy. All puppies, however, should eat three times a day until they are six months old; then they should be fed twice daily.

As described in chapter 8, you will tailor your feeding based on how much you are providing during training sessions. The younger the puppy the less you will feed at each feeding, and as your puppy grows, you will increase the amount based on weight. This is another reason to get your puppy established with a veterinarian. Your veterinarian will weigh your puppy and perform a body conditioning score, which will tell you if you are feeding correctly and if you need to adjust the amounts. Following are approximate amounts for different-sized puppies.

Toy and small breeds (e.g., Yorkshire terriers, Chihuahuas, Shih-Tzus, Toy Poodles, Maltese, etc.) should be fed approximately one-quarter to one-half cup of dry food three times a day (twice a day after six months old).

Medium breeds (e.g., Standard Schnauzers, Cocker and Springer spaniels, etc.) should be fed approximately one-half to three-quarter's cup of food three times daily (twice a day after six months old).

Large breeds (e.g., Labradors, Boxers, Dalmatians, etc.) should be fed approximately one-half to one cup three times daily (twice a day after six months old).

Extra-large breeds (e.g., Rottweilers, Giant Schnauzers, Great Danes, etc.) should be fed approximately one and a half to two coups three times daily (twice a day after six months old).

Of course, these are just estimates. Depending on the size, age, and activity level of your puppy, these amounts will be adjusted up or down and will be adjusted as your puppy becomes an adult.

As stated earlier, if your puppy is leaving food in the bowl, you are feeding too much; scale back until he is eating the entire bowl of food at each meal.

Treats

Many people like to give their puppy treats from time to time. Treats are fine to give to your puppy, but as with food, the amount and type you give is important. For instance, your puppy will not be getting proper nutrition if you are giving him so many treats that he does not eat his food. We have heard many people say "My dog doesn't like to eat his food," and upon investigation, we learn that the dog is getting a steady stream of treats throughout the day. Either the dog is not hungry from getting so many treats, or he is just holding out for the better-tasting goodie. Just as you would not allow your child to eat cookies and ice cream all day instead of a healthy dinner, the same goes for your new puppy. Treats are the equivalent to "junk food" and should be given sparingly

Commercial dog treats do not have enough nutrition to sustain a dog. They are never to be given in place of food. Just as with humans, if you eat too much junk food, you will have weight and health problems, however a treat now and then does not hurt. Most people feed their dog too many treats.

They think that giving the puppy treats is showing that you love them. However, your puppy would benefit more from a walk or a play session, and that builds a stronger bond than any treat ever could.

So, how many treats are good? With the Puppy Montessori program, you will be rewarding your puppy for good behavior throughout the day; giving any treats beyond this is not recommended. This is why we recommend using your puppy's kibble as a reward or using Natural Balance meat roll, which is a complete nutrition dog food, not a treat. If you absolutely want to give your puppy a "treat," you should limit it to one or two per day.

The type of treats you feed your puppy is important as well. Like dog food, there are many dog treats on the market. If you look at the ingredient list on most commercial dog treats, you will find many ingredients you cannot pronounce. As with human food, you want to feed treats that have the fewest of these ingredients. Many of these ingredients can cause skin and health problems in your pet over the years. If given too frequently, they can cause pancreatitis (inflammation of the pancreas that can lead to death).

We recommend feeding treats that are all natural with limited ingredients. To find these treats you may have to go to a pet bakery, a dog food specialty store, or order on line from a pet bakery rather than buying from the grocery store. At Super Mutts, we sell all natural dog bones that we make from human-quality ingredients, have no artificial colors or preservatives, and are safe to feed your pet. You can purchase these at www.supermutts.com. A portion of proceeds goes to help shelter animals, so you will be making your dog and a shelter dog happy!

We also recommend staying away from treats that look like plastic or rubber. These treats are the most processed treats you can purchase and not healthy. We also do not recommend buying any treats made in countries other than the United States. There have been many recalls on chicken jerky and other treats made in China. These treats have caused illness and death in some pets.

Many dogs enjoy vegetables as treats, and this is by far the best "treat" you can feed your dog. Many dogs will like carrots, apples, or green beans. You can also make your own dog treats. You can find recipes on the Internet and will know exactly what ingredients are in them.

Dogs should not be fed table scraps. By feeding your dog table scraps, you will create a dog that will not eat dog food, will beg at the table, and will become overweight and generally unhealthy. Many table scraps can make your dog sick with diarrhea, vomiting, and can cause pancreatitis.

 ALERT: There are many human foods that are dangerous or poisonous to your puppy; following is a list from the ASPCA of foods you should NEVER feed your dog.

Chocolate, coffee, caffeine

These products all contain substances called methylxanthines, which are found in cacao seeds, the fruit of the plant used to make coffee, and in the nuts of an extract used in some sodas. When ingested by pets, methylxanthines can cause vomiting and diarrhea, panting, excessive thirst and urination, hyperactivity, abnormal heart rhythm, tremors, seizures, and even death. Note that darker chocolate is more dangerous than milk chocolate. White chocolate has the lowest level of methylxanthines, while baking chocolate contains the highest.

Alcohol

Alcoholic beverages and food products containing alcohol can cause vomiting, diarrhea, decreased coordination, central nervous system depression, difficulty breathing, tremors, abnormal blood acidity, coma, and even death.

Avocado

The leaves, fruit, seeds, and bark of avocados contain persin, which can cause vomiting and diarrhea in dogs. Birds and rodents are especially sensitive to avocado poisoning, and can develop congestion, difficulty breathing, and fluid accumulation around the heart. Some ingestion may even be fatal.

Macadamia nuts

Macadamia nuts are commonly used in many cookies and candies. However, they can cause problems for your canine companion. These nuts have caused weakness, depression, vomiting, tremors, and hyperthermia in dogs.

Signs usually appear within twelve hours of ingestion and last approximately twelve to forty-eight hours.

Grapes and raisins

Although the toxic substance within grapes and raisins is unknown, these fruits can cause kidney failure. In pets that already have certain health problems, signs may be more dramatic.

Yeast dough

Yeast dough can rise and cause gas to accumulate in your pet's digestive system. This can be painful and can cause the stomach or intestines to rupture. Because the risk diminishes after the dough is cooked and the yeast has fully risen, pets can have small bits of bread as treats. However, these treats should not constitute more than 5 percent to 10 percent of your pet's daily caloric intake.

Raw/undercooked meat, eggs, and bones

Raw meat and raw eggs can contain bacteria such as *salmonella* and *E. coli* that can be harmful to pets. In addition, raw eggs contain an enzyme called avidin that decreases the absorption of biotin (a B vitamin), which can lead to skin and coat problems. Feeding your pet raw bones may seem like a natural and healthy option that might occur if your pet lived in the wild. However, this can be very dangerous for a domestic pet, which might choke on bones, or sustain a grave injury should the bone splinter and become lodged in or puncture your pet's digestive tract.

Xylitol

Xylitol is used as a sweetener in many products, including gum, candy, baked goods, and toothpaste. It can cause insulin release in most species, which can lead to liver failure. The increase in insulin leads to hypoglycemia (lowered sugar levels). Initial signs of toxicosis include vomiting, lethargy, and loss of coordination. Signs can progress to recumbency and seizures. Elevated liver enzymes and liver failure can be seen within a few days.

Onions, garlic, chives

These vegetables and herbs can cause gastrointestinal irritation and could lead to red blood cell damage. Although cats are more susceptible, dogs are also at risk if they consume a large enough amount. Toxicity is normally diagnosed through history, clinical signs, and microscopic confirmation of Heinz bodies. An occasional low dose, such as what might be found in pet foods or treats, likely will not cause a problem, but we recommend that you do NOT give your pets large quantities of these foods.

Milk

Because pets do not possess significant amounts of lactase (the enzyme that breaks down lactose in milk), milk and other milk-based products cause diarrhea or other digestive upset.

Salt

Large amounts of salt can produce excessive thirst and urination, or even sodium ion poisoning in pets. Signs that your pet may have eaten too many salty foods include vomiting, diarrhea, depression, tremors, elevated body temperature, seizures, and even death.

If you think your puppy has ingested any of these foods, you should call your veterinarian as soon as possible. You can also contact the ASPCA animal poison control center at (888) 426-4435.

RAW food diets

Raw food diets have become popular over the recent years and controversial. Racing dogs and sled dogs have been fed raw food diets for years. However, recently raw food diets have become more popular for the family pet. Supporters of raw food diets state the benefits include shinier coats, healthier skin, cleaner teeth, higher energy levels, and smaller stools.

Critics of raw food diets say the potential risks include threats to human and dog health from bacteria in raw meat, an unbalanced diet that may damage the health of dogs if given for an extended period, and the potential for whole bones to choke an animal, break teeth, or cause an internal puncture.

It has been reported that dogs with skin and coat problems have benefited greatly from switching to raw food diets.

Purchasing ingredients from the local grocer, you can prepare raw food diets. If you plan to prepare your own raw food diet, do your research, talk to your vet, and make sure your pet is getting all the required nutrition. There is a method to feeding raw food. Raw food diets are generally more expensive to feed and take more preparation than traditional commercial dog food. There are a number of companies that make prepackaged raw food diets to take the guesswork out of it. You cannot purchase these at the local grocer and will have to order them either over the Internet or at a specialty pet food retail store.

If your pet is eating traditional premium dog food and does not have any health problems, then switching to raw food is not necessary, but if you have a dog with health problems, especially skin or allergy issues, trying raw food diets cannot hurt and might just help.

Therefore, when it comes to feeding your new puppy, you want to feed the best puppy food you can afford, limit the number of treats, and stay away from feeding table scraps. If your puppy is having health issues or stomach upset, you may have to switch to another brand. Some dogs have intolerances to certain ingredients in food. Sometimes switching food can cause stomach upset as well. If you switch food, be sure to start by gradually mixing the new food in with the current food your puppy is eating until eventually he is eating just the new food. This applies when switching from puppy to adult dog food as well. Remember, the motto "you are what you eat" applies to your puppy as well. If you follow these basic guidelines, you should have a healthy puppy for years to come.

Chapter 13

Games to End

Resource Guarding and Food Aggression

Money will buy you a pretty good dog, but it won't buy the wag of his tail. ~ Henry Wheeler Shaw

Resource guarding and food aggression simply means that your dog guards things that he sees as a valuable resource, such as a toy or food. Many dogs have issues with resource guarding. When a dog resource guards, he will take the toy or bone, hold it with his mouth, and generally his feet. When anyone tries to take the item, he will stare, growl, show teeth, and if pushed will oftentimes bite.

There are different reasons as to why dogs become resource guarders. First and foremost is that it is a natural instinct for survival. In a wild dog pack, dogs have to guard food for survival. The fewer resources available, the more one has to guard those resources or go hungry. Therefore, resource guarding is a natural instinct that every dog possesses. Breeds that have harder mouths and high drive tend to be more resource guarding. Breeds with softer mouths, such as hunting breeds, tend to be less resource guarding.

Resource guarding can be taught. Many people unknowingly teach their dogs to resource guard through play. For instance, when a dog picks up a toy and you grab the toy and play tug, or encourage the dog to guard through growling while you act like you are going to take the toy or food away, you are "teaching" the dog to be a resource guarder. The dog learns that when he growls and grabs the toy, you back off and he wins.

Taking away resources and never giving them back can also create a dog that guards resources. If you never give the resource back or "trade" for an alternate resource, then the dog thinks he must guard it in fear of losing it.

Another reason dogs will guard resources is lack of leadership. A dog is not going to relinquish a valuable resource to a lower-ranking pack member.

Therefore, as you can see, there are several reasons your puppy may become a resource guarder. The good news is that there are several ways you can prevent this from ever becoming a problem.

You should always be able to take things from your dog's mouth without being bitten. If your dog gets into something it should not, such as a dead bird, poison, or something that could make it sick, you want to be able to take it from him quickly. Now is the time to teach your puppy to relinquish things to you when you ask.

By hand feeding your puppy through the Puppy Montessori program, you are already teaching that good things come from your hands. This will build trust and will create a good association with your hands and the puppy's food. To keep your puppy from becoming food aggressive follows these simple steps.

When feeding your puppy from a bowl, you should periodically reach down with your hands and put a few pieces of tasty treats in the bowl. This should be a high-value treat such as the cut-up beef roll or cut-up turkey hotdogs or something your puppy thinks is very tasty, even a small spoon full of canned food will work. This will teach your puppy that when your hands are near the food he gets extra treats. You should do this every time you feed your puppy. Eventually you will see your puppy take his face from the bowl and look toward your hand for the treat.

Once you have done the above exercise several times, you can then start picking up the food bowl while your puppy is eating. Place a tasty treat in the bowl and give it back to the puppy. Do this rather quickly, not keeping the food from the puppy too long. By doing this, your puppy will learn that when you take the bowl, he will get it back and it will have something even better in it. He will learn that you do not want to "take" his food from him but want to give him extra food instead. Everyone in the household should practice this exercise to make a good association for your puppy when people are around the food.

Drop it and leave it commands

Some of you may have adopted an older puppy or a puppy that shows some resource guarding behaviors. Through the drop it and leave it commands you will teach your puppy to relinquish items that he has in his possession or mouth, and to leave items alone that you do not want him to have.

The drop it game

As with any training exercise, have your treat pouch handy with tasty treats. Pick up a toy that your pet really likes and plays with frequently. Get the puppy interested by shaking and moving the toy. Once your puppy takes the toy in his mouth and does not want to relinquish it, hold a treat in front of his nose. When the puppy drops the toy, say "good dog" and give the treat. Immediately after this, give the toy back to the puppy and continue playing.

 Note: *It is important to give the toy back to the puppy after he drops it. If you keep the toy away from the puppy after he drops it, he will be less likely to drop it the next time. You want the puppy to know that after he drops the toy, play continues and does not abruptly end.*

At this time you can also incorporate the "take it" or "get it" command. Before you give the puppy the toy to continue playing simply say "take it" and give him the toy.

Continue the above exercise several times until your dog is quickly releasing the toy when you show him the treat. Once the puppy is releasing the toy several times, you will then add "drop it."

Show the treat when the puppy releases the toy, say "drop it," and give the puppy praise and a treat. Repeat several times throughout the day. Eventually you will say "drop it" while the treat is still in the treat pouch where the puppy cannot see it. Once the puppy releases the toy on the "drop it" command, praise, treat, and continue play as above. You should then start adding the "drop it" command whenever your puppy has something in his mouth. If done frequently enough you will be able to tell your dog to "drop it" anytime he picks up something like a sock, shoe, dead animal, spoiled food, cell phone, the television remote control, or anything potentially dangerous.

As with training any command, you want to reward the behavior with a treat every time during the learning phase. Once your puppy is dropping the toy every time you give the command, you can give fewer food rewards. Giving the toy back and playing with the puppy after the pet drops it, is reward enough for most dogs. However, do not rush the process.

NOTE: *Many people give up on food rewards too soon. When training any command, the goal is to develop a habit. Your puppy needs to repeat the behavior several times and be rewarded frequently before the behavior becomes automatic. Many people phase out the food reward before they have developed an automatic behavior. Remember, ten packs of turkey hot dogs are a lot cheaper than one pair of good running shoes or pumps! Even after your pet is an adult and drops something on command, you should still periodically reward the behavior with a tasty treat.*

The leave it game

The "leave it" game is very important in that it stops your dog from ever putting something potentially dangerous or unwanted in his mouth. Puppies are very curious, and if something is dropped on the floor, they will generally run over to it and may pick it up. With the "leave it" command you can stop this in an instant. With the "leave it" command you are teaching your puppy to ignore something it wants and look at you. You can also use this command when your puppy wants to do something like chasing a cat or bird.

To train the "leave it" command you will need some regular dry kibble or a dry dog bone, your treat pouch and your puppy on leash. In one hand have a few pieces of dry kibble; in the other hand have some very tasty food reward. Place the kibble or bone on the floor, not allowing your puppy to get to it. When your puppy goes toward the kibble gently pull him away while luring him with the tasty treat in the other hand. Reward and say "good dog!" Pick up the kibble and repeat several times without using the command.

Once the puppy is looking to you readily and leaving the food on the floor, incorporate "leave it." The food reward should be much tastier than the food on the floor, or this will not work. Repeat this several times until your puppy no longer needs you to lure him away from the dry kibble and looks up immediately when given the command. Once your puppy has learned the command, then you can use it with other things your puppy tries to pick up or go after. Remember to never give this or any command unless you have something tasty to reward the puppy with, and never give the puppy the food on the floor during this lesson. You do not want your puppy to think he can "leave it" and then "take it."

Once your puppy is performing the "leave it" command readily, you can use the command when out on a walk, as well. When your puppy tries to lunge toward something like a bird, cat, or other animal, say "leave it" and lure him toward you with the food reward. Make sure your reward is a high-value reward and praise, praise, praise when your puppy leaves the wanted object and comes to you. This is a very difficult thing for the puppy to do and demands the highest form of reward. This will teach your puppy that when you say "leave it" he needs to look to you and not continue going toward the wanted object.

If at any point your puppy is not performing the command, it could be that your reward is not valuable enough for him to leave what he wants, or you have trained too long and he has lost interest in the game. You should increase the value of the reward to something tastier and remember to keep the sessions short and practice often throughout the day.

By playing these games early and often with your puppy you will create an adult dog that will drop or leave any object and will not have issues with resource guarding.

Chapter 14

Toys and Chews

A puppy plays with every pup he meets, but an old dog has few associates. ~ Josh Billings

Just as children need toys, so do puppies. Toys provide not only mental and physical stimulation for your puppy but also keep them from becoming bored. Toys also keep your puppy entertained while providing you with a needed break. With the Puppy Montessori program, the puppy should always have toys and chews while in the nursery. Toys come in many varieties such as plush, latex, rubber, and plastic. They come in many shapes, sizes, and prices. There are interactive toys as well that help keep your puppy's mind stimulated. The types of toys you provide will depend on your puppy. Some puppies are destructive chewers with hard mouths, so plush toys will not last long. Other puppies, such as retrievers or spaniels, have softer mouths and do well with plush toys. On the following pages, we list the toys that have been the most popular with our dogs as well as some of the indestructible ones. It is not wise to purchase children's stuffed animals for your pet. Many of human toys contain parts and fillings that can be easily chewed and swallowed by your puppy, causing possible bowel obstruction.

There are some people that believe you should not provide your dog with multiple toys for them to have whenever they want. Their thinking is that you should give the toys when you want your dog to play and you should put them away when you are done playing. They say that this shows the dog that you own the toys not the dog. We believe that this kind of thinking makes the toy a more "valuable" resource and can cause potential resource guarding, especially in a multiple-dog household. We have found that in having a "pack" of dogs and running a doggy day care that the more toys the better. More toys in a multiple-dog household or day care setting minimize resource guarding over any one toy. Now we will say that all dogs need to know that you own the resources, not them. By implementing the drop it and leave it commands you have already taught your puppy that he is to relinquish any resource you tell him to. (Hence, all resources belong to you.) If two puppies or dogs seem to have an issue with guarding a toy from others, simply remove that toy from the equation.

We will also say that if you want your dog to be calm and relaxed when people come to your home, it is not a good idea for friends to play with your puppy. By doing this, your puppy will think that every time people come over it is time to get excited and play. They will continue this into adulthood. We ourselves have been guilty of doing this, and it is a hard habit to break. Remember our motto:

"It is easier to train good behaviors than undo bad ones."

Many people want their dog to be calm in the house. In this case you should allow your puppy to play with toys on his own or chew a bone, but you should limit playing fetch or tug to outside. This way the puppy learns that we play calmly in the house and play in a more excited fashion outside. It is also important for you to be the one to initiate play and to end play. You should not play with a dog simply because he brings you a toy. For a toy-obsessed dog, this will create a dog that is constantly bringing you toys. You should either make him perform something for you such as "sit" before you play or better yet, you should ignore him at that time.

With forty-two to forty-four teeth present in adult dogs, twelve incisors, four canine teeth, sixteen premolars, and ten to twelve molars, and puppies having twenty-eight deciduous teeth, dogs are meant to chew! Bones and chews provide your puppy with mental stimulation and help to aid in teething and teeth cleaning. By providing the correct chews throughout your puppy's life, you will spend less money on teeth cleaning at the veterinarian.

There has been some opposition about letting dogs chew bones. The reasons sighted are that bones can break teeth, can become lodged in the throat or intestine or cause bowel obstruction—and, yes, all these things can happen if you give the wrong type of bones to your puppy or adult dog. People who feed raw food diets feed certain bones without incidence. We have provided our dogs with the bones listed below for many years and have only had one incident of a broken tooth. We also have not needed to take our dogs to the vet for teeth cleaning. Into old age, our dogs' teeth have no tartar.

We do not recommend giving your puppy bones from the table; cooked bones and poultry bones should never be given because of potential splintering. Size matters as well. Your puppy should not be given small bones that could be swallowed completely. All bones should be given with supervision, and if small pieces break off they should be discarded. You also should not feed too many bones or bones that are small enough for your dog to eat in one sitting.

 ALERT: We do not recommend any chew made of rawhide. Even though rawhide does not break or splinter, when chewed on it becomes soft and forms a ball that can be easily swallowed and ingested. We have seen many dogs vomit balls of rawhide the size that could easily cause obstruction.

If you are apprehensive about feeding bones, there are alternatives on the market that we have listed below that also provide the similar teeth cleaning ability. In our experience, however, nothing is more preferable to a dog than a nice natural bone to chew on.

With so many dog toys and chews on the market, you have a wide array of options to entertain your puppy. However, not all toys or chews are good for your puppy, and some can even be harmful. Throughout our years raising dogs and running a "dog" business, we have tried and tested many different toys and chews and have come up with a small list of toys that are the most preferred. We have rated their durability from low to high. We are also providing a list of preferred chews.

Toys

Plush toys—low durability. Plush toys are toys made of soft fabric stuffed with some form of fiberfill generally looking like a stuffed animal and oftentimes have a squeaker inside. They come in a variety of shapes, sizes, colors, and prices. Plush toys are great for small dogs or dogs with soft mouths. If you have a harder-mouthed dog, such as a Rottweiler or bulldog, plush toys are a waste of money. Hard-mouthed dogs tend to chew and shred plush toys in a minimal amount of time. In all our years of experience, we have only recently found two plush toys that hold up to hard-mouthed chewers. Note, ultimately they will fail, but they last significantly longer than the average plush toy. These are Kygen plush puppies and the Kong Dodo. All dogs are different; however, the only way to determine if your dog will destroy a plush toy is to provide him with one and see what happens. We had a Boxer that loved teddy bears and would not destroy plush toys. It is important to pick up the fiberfill immediately if your dog shreds a plush toy. Fiberfill can cause a bowel obstruction if ingested.

Stuffingless dog toys—low to medium durability. Basically a stuffingless dog toy is a plush toy that has no stuffing. These do tend to last longer than a stuffed toy for many dogs, and they like throwing them around. Some dogs still chew off the legs or tail, however.

Latex toys—low durability. Latex toys are rubber dog toys that come in a variety of sizes and shapes and contain a squeaker. Latex toys are generally inexpensive. Many dogs love latex toys and will prance around for hours squeaking them, which can become annoying to some people. Many softer latex toys are easy for dogs to destroy. If your dog shreds plush toys, chances are he will destroy latex toys as well.

Rope bone toys—medium to high durability. Rope bone toys are a great toy for any puppy or dog. They come in many different sizes and are quite durable. Dogs enjoy chewing on the knots at the end and they make it easy to play tug.

Kongs—high durability. Kongs are a hard rubber toy with a hole in the bottom for stuffing treats into. Kongs are virtually indestructible and come in different sizes. Kongs are a great toy to give to your puppy when you leave him in his kennel for any length of time or want him to settle down. You can stuff the Kong with kibble, treats, peanut butter, canned food, or a combination of these. We highly recommend getting a couple of Kongs to put in your puppy's nursery.

Rubber toys from JW Pet—high durability JW Pet has a number of rubber toys that are more durable than most, and a majority of dogs like to play with them. Our dogs have had some of these toys for years and they are still in good shape. They come in many shapes and sizes

Of course, the standard tennis ball is always a great toy for your new puppy. Some dogs will shred the outer lining of a tennis ball and swallow it, so it is good to play fetch with but not leave with your puppy while unattended.

Chews

Nyla bone chews—Nyla bone makes a wide array of chews designed with durable nylon for strong chewers. They come in many different flavors and will last quite a long time. No pieces can break off so they are safe to leave with your puppy when unattended. Some of them come with little stubbles on them to help aid in teeth cleaning.

Beef bones—You can purchase beef shank bones, knuckle bones, femur bones, or kneecaps for smaller dogs. They come with some marrow and gristle left on the bone, and dogs LOVE them. However, they can be messy at first, so do not put them on white carpet! They last a long time so you get your money's worth. We highly recommend them. Dogs tend to gnaw on them and whittle them away. It is rare that they will break pieces off but it is possible, so you should monitor your puppy and remove any broken pieces. Once these bones are chewed clean, they can last for years. We have always provided these to our dogs, and it is the chew they prefer, especially after eating a meal.

When these bones are new, some dogs eat quite a bit off them, which can cause stomach upset. In that case, you should give them to your puppy for limited amounts of time until the gristle and marrow are gone. Once the gristle and marrow are gone, you can leave them down continuously.

Keep in mind that these bones will be the most prized resource for your puppy. If you have established the "drop it" game as mentioned in the previous chapter, you should not have a problem with resource guarding. If you have multiple dogs, it is always recommended that you have enough bones for each dog. If you only have one bone for multiple dogs, you are asking for trouble. Our dogs have multiple bones down at all times and share them readily.

Deer Antlers—Deer antlers are another great chew for your puppy. They are durable, and do not break. We have found that some dogs love them and others do not seem interested in them. It does not hurt to have a few around.

When it comes to toys and chews, the key is to provide your puppy with a wide array of options to choose from. This will keep your new puppy's mind occupied and will help curb boredom.

You can purchase all these toys or chews through our website at www.supermutts.com. Similar to what we stated about dog treats, a few well-selected dog toys or bones are still cheaper than a pair of running shoes or new furniture.

Playing tug

We want to take this opportunity to discuss playing tug with your puppy. Dogs love to play tug. They do it with each other and with humans. There are a couple of different thoughts on playing tug with a dog. Some trainers say you should not play tug because it creates dominance in a dog, and others say you should play tug in that it teaches the dog to listen while excited and builds stronger bonds.

Tug is a fun game to play with your puppy if done correctly. There are right and wrong ways to play tug, and not all dogs should play tug. By teaching your puppy the "drop it" command, you are establishing the correct way to play tug. We do not recommend playing tug with your puppy until he has an understanding of the "drop it" command. With a young puppy, you do not want to tug too hard, puppies have baby teeth, some of them loose, and playing tug may pull them out.

When playing tug with your puppy, choose a toy that is long enough to keep your hands away from the puppy's mouth, such as a long rope toy. As with all play, the human should always initiate the game and end the game. With one hand on each end of the toy, show it to your puppy and say "take it." Once the puppy takes it, you can tug on the end. After a few minutes of play, stop tugging, and while holding the toy completely still say "drop it." Once the puppy drops the toy say "good." You can give a treat at this time. Give your puppy some other commands such as "sit" or "down." Once your puppy performs these commands say "take it" and continue play. This will teach your puppy to listen to you even when he is excited or engaged in play. By holding the toy still and giving the drop it command you are teaching your puppy that play is to end when the toy is still. Eventually you will not have to say "drop it." The puppy will learn to do so automatically once you hold the toy still. You can also let your puppy "win" the tug game on occasion as long as you can give the "drop it" command and continue play.

If at any time during play, your puppy puts his teeth on you (accidentally or otherwise), say "ouch" in a loud voice and walk away with the toy for thirty seconds or so. This will teach your puppy if he puts teeth on you, play ends.

If you see that your puppy gets too excited or aggressive or will not perform the commands, you may want to find another form of play such as "fetch." Some dogs also do not enjoy the game of tug and will not engage in it; in that case, another form of play will be more rewarding. Tug is a game you can play with your puppy if you establish the correct way to do it from the beginning. When dogs play tug they can get very aggressive, using their whole body to grab, hold, and pull. We would not recommend playing tug with an adult dog that you are unfamiliar with. By starting your puppy out early on the correct way to play tug, you will be able to play tug with him throughout his adult life.

Teaching retrieve (fetch)

For those dogs that do not play tug, retrieving is a game that most dogs love to engage in. Dogs with high prey drive love to retrieve, such as the herding breeds, terriers, and the hunting breeds. For a few dogs however, retrieving does not come natural. In our experience, we have seen retrievers that do not "retrieve" and have had to be taught.

Retrieving is unlocking your puppy's "prey" drive. Dogs with high prey drive tend to have natural "ball drive" as well. Teaching retrieve also teaches the dog to fetch and bring things to you and is a necessity if you want to do any type of service dog training with your dog in the future. Teaching the retrieve should be done after your dog has been taught the recall or "come" command and the "drop it" command. Again, as with all play, the human should initiate the game and end the game.

Have your treat pouch handy and get your puppy interested in a ball by moving it around until he gets excited. Play the "drop it" game a few times then roll the ball a short distance from you, many puppies will automatically go after the ball. Once the puppy has the ball in his mouth, say "come." When the puppy gets to you, say "drop it" then praise, praise, praise, and reward with a treat. Repeat this several times until the puppy is performing this readily. Once the puppy is retrieving readily, you can then use a terms such as "get it" or "fetch" when you throw the ball and "bring it" when he picks the ball up to bring it back to you. This will teach your dog what the terms "get it" or "fetch" and "bring it" mean and will allow you to have your dog "fetch" and "bring" whatever he has in his mouth in the future.

It is important to play the retrieve game in short increments once or twice a day and then put the ball away. By making it a very fun game for your puppy and doing it only occasionally, you will build ball drive in your puppy.

Some dogs have a high ball drive and will catch on quickly without much training. Others will take a little longer. If you have a puppy that does not seem interested in the ball, you can use marker training to help by breaking the game up into smaller steps.

Place the ball on the floor. Have your treats ready. Roll the ball around a little with your hand. If the puppy looks at it, say "good" and reward with a treat. Do this every time the puppy looks at the ball or moves toward the ball. Repeat frequently. Once the puppy catches on to looking at the ball, then point to the ball and only reward when he touches the ball with his nose or even with a paw. Remember to say the marker word "good" before you give the reward. Eventually you will reward only when the puppy is picking up the ball. Once the puppy is picking up the ball, then you can work on retrieving as above. Some puppies are more interested in a toy other than a ball. In this case, use whatever toy your puppy is interested in. You will have better luck teaching the retrieve with a toy your puppy is fond of.

ALERT: It is important to note that dogs with high ball drive will bring the ball to you repeatedly. It is important not to engage in retrieve with your dog unless YOU initiate and end the play. With a high ball drive dog, by throwing the ball every time the dog brings it to you, you may create a dog that is ball obsessed.

As with the game of tug, if your puppy becomes overly excited, you should have him sit before you throw the ball. If the puppy tries to jump up and nip at you or steal the ball in an aggressive manner, mark the behavior with a loud "ouch!" and stop play. Play should be used only as a reward for good behavior. If you play with your puppy when he is excited or aggressive, you are reinforcing that behavior. Remember our motto: **"It is easier to train good behaviors than undo bad ones."**

Every experience your puppy has is a learning opportunity. Even in play, you are teaching your puppy desired behaviors. Remember that the human should initiate and end all play. Playing with your puppy correctly will build strong bonds between the two of you and will make the puppy more willing to perform commands when asked.

Chapter 15

Big Dog

A leader is one who knows the way, goes the way, and shows the way.

~John C. Maxwell

What does it take to be the big dog, the leader? Not in size but in temperament. After all, size has nothing to do with being the "big dog" in the dog world. There are dogs the size of Rottweilers that are the "big dog," but there are also dogs the size of Chihuahuas that are the "big dog."

We want to take this time to talk about two terms that humans often misuse and misunderstand. One is the term "alpha," the other is the term "NILIF," or nothing in life is free. As dog trainers, we hear many people use both of these terms but when questioned on what they mean, they do not fully understand or sometimes have no clue what they really mean.

Alpha

In our dog training, we seldom use the term "alpha." We also never tell people they need to be the "alpha." When we first meet people to help with their dogs we always discuss leadership and the importance of being a good leader to your dog. In our experience, when people hear the term "alpha," they assume it means being aggressive or dominant over your dog. That you should "force" your dog to submit to you. This thinking is the furthest from the truth.

In social animals, the alpha is the individual in the community with the highest rank. Male or female individuals or both can be alphas, depending on their species. Where one male and one female fulfill this role, they are referred to as the alpha pair. Other animals in the same social group may exhibit deference or other symbolic signs of respect particular to their species toward the alpha or alphas. In hierarchal social animals, alphas usually gain preferential access to food and other desirable items or activities, though the extent of this social effect varies widely by species. Male and female alphas may gain preferential access to sex or mates, and in some species, only alphas or an alpha pair is permitted to reproduce.

Alphas may achieve their status by means of superior physical prowess or through social efforts and building alliances within the group.

The position of alpha also changes in some species, usually through a physical fight between a dominant and subordinate animal. Such fights may or may not be to the death, with relevant behavior varying between circumstance and species.

Many people use the term "alpha" to tell us that their dog's aggressive or out-of-control behavior is because he is the "alpha." This also is untrue. In fact, if your dog is acting outwardly aggressive or out of control, chances are it is because he senses no leadership and has not been provided with rules by you, the human. Dogs are self-serving opportunists, if you allow them to be bossy and it works for them, they will continue to do so. A bossy dog is a bossy dog, not an alpha dog.

In the dog world, there are only two positions, the leader or the follower. If you are not one, you are the other. Most dogs are not born "alpha" dogs. If they sense no leadership in the pack, they will automatically try to fill the role. If they are not a born "alpha dog," they will be terrible at it and you will see aggressive or fearful behaviors. A true "alpha" dog is rarely aggressive. If you are ever in the presence of a true "alpha" dog, you will see that he commands respect by calm assertiveness, not aggression and certainly not severe aggression unless the situation merits, such as a threat to his life.

A true alpha dog does not need to act aggressively, because everyone in the pack knows he is the alpha or leader and will respect his authority based on his energy within the pack. The relationship is based on trust and respect. Others will rarely challenge his authority. He can give a simple glance and they know not to mess with him. Not necessarily because he was aggressive toward them, but because they understand the intention with a simple look, that if they pushed him he would correct them and they would lose....period. When an alpha dog enters into a pack of dogs, he will let them know his position simply by the way he walks into the group. He generally will enter without sniffing anyone and will be aloof to other dogs around him. Other dogs will often follow the "alpha"; dog the alpha rarely follows the rest.

The picture above is of the alpha male and alpha female dogs of our pack before they passed away. George and Sonora. George was never overly aggressive toward any of our pack of four or the hundreds of dogs we see in our business. He walked with self-assurance and head held high. When we brought in a dog for evaluation, we would use George and Sonora for the evaluation. We used the two of them for their ability to always be aloof and ignore other dogs.

George never had to become aggressive with our other pack members. When we brought home our bulldog puppy Rudy, he would often approach George if George was chewing a bone. As Rudy would approach the bone, George would give him a look. If he continued, George would curl his lip and occasionally growl. If Rudy continued to push it, George would quickly and accurately bite Rudy on his face, hard enough to make him yelp and walk away. The next time Rudy approached, all George had to do was give the look. Rudy would take heed. However, there were times when George was chewing a bone or toy and would let Rudy take it because he was not that interested in it any longer. Being alpha does not mean being a tyrant. It means being a leader, being fair, and setting rules and boundaries. The other dogs always knew when they could or could not take something the alpha pair had.

Sonora was clearly the alpha female of the dog pack. She would stand her ground by growling and showing teeth if she disapproved. She was the more vocal of the two and used it to her advantage. The other dogs would take heed and not push her. She also would share resources and would play with the others.

It became startlingly clear to us that George and Sonora were the pack leaders of the dog pack when they both died in the same week. Our pack used to hang out in our backyard, which they had access to through a doggie door. We would always find them lying on our deck or under a bush or tree. Once George and Sonora died, the two remaining dogs, Bentley and Rudy seemed lost. They stuck closer to us and went outside only to go to the bathroom. To this day, they do not use the backyard as they did when George and Sonora were alive. Neither Rudy nor Bentley is a pack leader.

Now, the reason we say that George and Sonora were the leaders of the DOG pack is because even though they were the leaders of the dogs, they respected us as leaders of them. They would rarely challenge our commands and would allow us to take anything from them. Not because we intimidated them by using forceful techniques, but because we established a leadership program with them—a fair, consistent leadership program based on trust and respect.

By using the Puppy Montessori program and establishing clear rules and boundaries, you are teaching your puppy what is acceptable in the pack and what is not, which builds respect. By rewarding good behavior and controlling the situations your puppy is in, you are building trust. This puts you in the leadership role. For example, If you do not want your dog on the furniture, you let him know by either never letting him on the furniture or by directing him off of the furniture and rewarding him for lying on his own bed. These daily rules are what will establish you as the pack leader.

NILIF (nothing in life is free)

We cannot talk about leadership without talking about the NILIF program. NILIF simply means, "Nothing in life is free," and it means just that.

NILIF is a consistent methodology that is based on action/reaction. Basically it means that your puppy has to do something before he gets something he wants. Where people fail at this concept is by allowing the dog to make all the decisions on his own. By making all the decisions on his own, he then assumes he is the leader. If he is not a born leader, this is where you will see issues such as insecurity or dominance. For instance, your dog wants to jump on the furniture, and he does so anytime the mood strikes. If he wants to play ball, he brings you the ball, and you throw it. He wants to be petted, he nudges your hand, and you pet him. He wants to eat, he barks at you at dinnertime, and you feed him. All these things are the dog telling you to do something, and you do it. Bingo, in his mind, he must be the leader. This will also lead to a bossy dog.

The NILIF program was designed to put rules and boundaries in place to let your dog know that you are the leader of him, not the other way around. The first thing is to end all attention on demand. When your dog comes to you and nudges you to pet him or brings you a toy to play with, you ignore him. The only time you pet or play with your dog is when YOU initiate it. If he is sitting or lying away from you, call him to you and pet or play with him. Before you feed your dog or play with your dog he is to perform a task such as "sit" or "down." If he wants to get on the furniture or bed (and you allow him on the furniture), he should have to ask by coming to you and sitting before you give the command to get on the furniture. If he wants to go outside, he should sit and wait before doing so.

So you see, for everything the dog wants from you, he first must perform an action to get the reward he wants. Remember the program is called **NOTHING** in life is free. It is not called **SOME** things in life are free and that is where most people fall short on this program. Some people will say they are implementing the NILIF program by making their dog sit before feeding, but they still pet the dog or give attention on demand. This is not NILIF.

Many people tend to be overly affectionate to their dogs. In fact, many of the problems we see in dogs stem from people who give their dogs too much free-flowing affection. We are not saying you should never be affectionate to your dog; we are saying you should not be overly affectionate. Too much affection can create a dog that senses no leadership and oftentimes creates an anxious or nervous dog or a dog that is aggressive or dominant. Your dog should always perform some task before getting affection and should never be allowed to demand affection.

Understand this is just a primer for the NILIF concept, not the complete program or description. Again, as with any training program, you must be consistent. If you allow your dog to jump up on the furniture or demand attention on one day, and not on another, you will be confusing the dog. In a dog pack, the rules do not change on a daily basis. If your rules change daily, your dog will be unsure about what those rules are, which will lead to confusion and distrust. Be consistent!

In conclusion, Raising a puppy is never an easy endeavor but if done right can be less frustrating than doing it wrong. The Puppy Montessori program is designed to help take the frustration out of puppy ownership, creating a better bond between human and dog that can last a lifetime, if not yours, definitely your dog's.

Following are the twelve key components to the Puppy Montessori program:

Choosing the right puppy—It is "critical" to understand which puppy is right for you. Do your homework; raising a puppy should not begin with an impulse decision. **(Chapter 1)**

Understanding developmental levels—Puppies are like children. Understand that they are going to go through different phases of development. It is important for you to understand how to correctly respond to these phases in your puppy's development. **(Chapter 2)**

Communicating—Do not talk too much! It is important not to use words until you understand and establish proper communication with your puppy. **(Chapter 3)**

Setting up a nursery—Environmental controls are critical to your puppy's development and the relationship you will establish with your puppy. The goal is to help set up you and your puppy for success. **(Chapter 4)**

Potty training—Proper potty training will make or break your relationship with your puppy. Potty training issues are the number one reason puppies are rehomed. **(Chapter 5)**

Socializing—Socialize early and socialize often using proper techniques. **(Chapter 6)**

Leash walking—Leash = Love. The leash is the artery to your puppy's experience in the outside world. Dogs have four legs and are meant to walk. **(Chapter 7)**

Obedience—Train early, Train often! Obedience is the heart of a healthy human/dog relationship. **(Chapter 8)**

<u>Curbing destructive behaviors</u>—**It is easier to train good behaviors than undo bad ones!** Do not give too much freedom too soon. **(Chapter 9)**

<u>Health and wellness</u>—A healthy dog starts as a healthy puppy. Proper nutrition, grooming, and vaccinations are the foundations to a happy, healthy dog. **(Chapters 10, 11, 12)**

<u>Proper play</u>—Owning a puppy is not a game. Your puppy is constantly learning, even through play. Understand how to properly play with your puppy. **(Chapters 13 and 14)**

<u>Leadership is the key</u>—Become the big dog: understanding alpha and NILIF. **(Chapter 15)**

Appendix A

Works Consulted

www.aspca.org Page 73 - Information on distemper/ Page 79 – Information on ticks/ Page 81 – Information on heartworm/ Page 82 – Information on Spaying/neutering

www.doberman.org Page 18 – Information on adolescence

www.humanesociety.org

www.mixedbreedclubca.org – Page 47 - Definition of competition obedience

http://psychology.about.com/od/eindex/g/extinction.htm. Pages 61, 62, 63 - Definition of extinction burst

www.petmd.com Pages 74, 75, 76 - information on Parvo, Rabies, Bordetella/ Page 80 – Information on internal parasites

www.vetinfo.com Page 74 – information on Canine hepatitis

www.perfectpuppycare.com Page 75 – Information on Parainfluenza

http://vetmedicine.about.com Page 76 - Leptospirosis

www.nationalpetpharmacy.com Page 77 – Coronavirus

www.vetwellcare.com Page 77 - Vaccination table

http://en.wikipedia.org – Page 105 – Definition of Alpha

www.akc.org – for STAR puppy classes

http://www.humanesociety.org/issues/pet_overpopulation/tips/afford_spay_neuter.html?credit=web_id83576973 – For low cost spay/neuter finder

www.pets.webmd.com

www.petfinder.com

www.k9deb.com

www.leospetcare.com

Appendix B

Dog Food Ratings and Glossary

Here are dog food ratings for many of the most popular dog foods on the market today.

Alpo Prime Cuts / Score 81 C
Artemis Large/Medium Breed Puppy / Score 114 A+
Authority Harvest Baked / Score 116 A+
Authority Harvest Baked Less Active / Score 93 B
Beowulf Back to Basics / Score 101 A+
Bil-Jac Select / Score 68 F
Blackwood 3000 Lamb and Rice / Score 83 C
Blue Buffalo Chicken and Rice / Score 106 A+
Burns Chicken and Brown Rice / Score 107 A+
Canidae / Score 112 A+
Chicken Soup Senior / Score 115 A+
Diamond Maintenance / Score 64 F
Diamond Lamb Meal & Rice / Score 92 B
Diamond Large Breed 60+ Formula / Score 99 A
Diamond Performance / Score 85 C
Dick Van Patten's Natural Balance Ultra Premium / Score 122 A+
Dick Van Patten's Natural Balance Venison and Brown Rice / Score 106 A+
Dick Van Patten's Duck and Potato / Score 106 A+
EaglePack Holistic / Score 102 A+ Eagle Pack Holistic Chicken / Score 114 A+
Eagle Pack Natural / Score 94 A
Eagle Pack Large and Giant Breed Puppy Food / Score 94 A
Eukanuba Adult / Score 81 C
Eukanuba Puppy / Score 79 C
Flint River Senior / Score 101 A+
Foundations / Score 106 A+
Hund-n-Flocken Adult Dog (lamb) by Solid Gold / Score 93 B
Iams Lamb Meal & Rice Formula Premium / Score 73 D
Innova Dog / Score 114 A+
Innova Evo / Score 114 A+
Innova Large Breed Puppy / Score 122 A+
Kirkland Signature Chicken, Rice, and Vegetables / Score 110 A+
Member's Mark Chicken and Rice / Score 84 C

Merrick Wilderness Blend / Score 127 A+
Nature's Recipe / Score 100 A
Nature's Recipe Healthy Skin Venison and Rice / Score 116 A+
Nature's Variety Raw Instinct / Score 122 A+
Nutra Nuggets Super Premium Lamb Meal and Rice / Score 81 C
Nutrience Junior Medium Breed Puppy / Score 101 A+
Nutrisource Lamb and Rice / Score 87 B
Nutro Max Adult / Score 93 B
Nutro Natural Choice Lamb and Rice / Score 98 A
Nutro Natural Choice Large Breed Puppy / Score 87 B
Nutro Natural Choice Puppy Wheat Free / Score 86 B
Nutro Natural Choice Senior / Score 95 A
Nutro Ultra Adult / Score 104 A+
Pet Gold Adult with Lamb & Rice / Score 23 F
Premium Edge Chicken, Rice and Vegetables Adult Dry / Score 109 A+
Pro Nature Puppy / Score 80 C
Pro Plan Natural Turkey & Barley / Score 103 A+
Pro Plan Sensitive Stomach / Score 94 A
Purina Beneful / Score 17 F
Purina Dog / Score 62 F
Purina Come-n-Get It / Score 16 F
Purina One Large Breed Puppy / Score 62 F
Royal Canin Boxer / Score 103 A+
Royal Canin Bulldog / Score 100 A+
Royal Canin Natural Blend Adult / Score 106 A+
Science Diet Advanced Protein Senior 7+ / Score 63 F
Science Diet for Large Breed Puppies / Score 69 F
Sensible Choice Chicken and Rice / Score 97 A
Solid Gold / Score 99 A
Summit / Score 99 A
Timberwolf Organics Wild & Natural Dry / Score 120 A+
Timberwolf Organic Lamb and Vegetable / Score 136 A+
Wellness Super5 Mix Chicken / Score 110 A+
Wellness Super5Mix Senior Dry Dog 15 lb. Bag / Score 110 A+
Wolfking Adult Dog (Bison) by Solid Gold / Score 97 A

Glossary of terms used in dog food

Animal Digest: This is the dry by-product of rendered meat. During rendering, all usable animal parts (including fetal tissues and glandular wastes) are heated in vats, and the liquid is separated from the dry meal. This meal is covered with charcoal and labeled "unfit for human consumption" before processing it into pet food. Digest can also include intestines, as well as the contents of those intestines, such as stool, bile, parasites, and chemicals.

Animal Fat and Tallow: Animal fat is a "generic" fat source that most often consists of rendered animal fat, rancid restaurant grease, or other oils that are deemed inedible for humans. Tallow is low-quality hard white fat that most animals find hard to digest, not to mention the cardiac risks resulting.

Chemical Preservatives: Chemical preservatives include BHA (butylated hydroxyanisole), BHT (butylated hydroxytolulene), propyl gallate, propylene glycol (also used in automotive antifreeze and is suspected of causing red blood cell damage), and ethoxquin. They are all potentially cancer-causing agents that your pets are eating every day.

Chicken By-products: These are ground parts from poultry carcasses such as feet, heads, feathers, intestines, necks, and undeveloped eggs. They can included any rendered material.

Corn Products: Corn products, including corn meal, gluten, and grits, are cheap, allergy-causing fillers, and are very difficult for animals to digest.

Food Fragments: Lower-end by-products of the food manufacturing process. Examples include wheat bran and brewers' rice, which are a waste product of the alcohol industry.

Ground Whole Grain Sorghum: The feed value of grain sorghum is similar to corn. It is grown primarily as a feed grain for livestock.

Meat and Bone Meal: "Meat" and bone meal are inexpensive sources of animal protein. Note that these companies do not clarify the source of "meat," nor is it human-grade meat. The protein in meat meal containing a large amount of processed bone may not be digestible and fail to provide adequate nutrition.

Meat Based: A label that say "meat based" may also include blood vessels, tendons, organs and other parts of the rendered animal. Note again that these companies do not clarify the source of "meat," nor are they human-grade meat products.

Meat By-products: Pet-grade meat by-products consist of organs and parts not desired or not fit for human consumption. This can include organs, bones, blood, and fatty tissue. It can also include brains, feet, heads, intestines, and any other internal parts. Unbelievably, *by-products can also contain cancerous or diseased tissue containing parasites and euthanized animals.*

About the Authors

Kenneth and Cindy Quigley are the co-owners of Super Mutts. Super Mutts is a canine retreat and rehabilitation center located in Apache Junction, Arizona. Cindy Quigley has been an animal lover all her life, and from a young age she knew her life's work would be spent in the service of animals. She grew up with animals and trained her first dog at age seventeen. In 1984 she became a veterinary technician. In 1985 she became a professional pet stylist, apprenticing under a groomer of twenty-plus years. She groomed professionally for eight years, and in 1993 made a career change and became a registered nurse. During that time she continued building and training a pack of dogs at home and studying animal behavior. She has worked in grooming shops, boarding facilities, and veterinary hospitals, all of which taught her how to read canine body language and understand dog handling. Throughout her eleven years of nursing, she felt something missing and decided to follow her heart. In 2003, Cindy and her husband, Kenneth, opened Super Mutts. Super Mutts is a canine retreat that offers training, boarding, day care, and grooming.

Kenneth Quigley has been an animal lover all his life, caring for anything his parents would let him bring home. He has personally cared for and trained dogs since he was a teenager. Early in life he knew that animal care would play an important role in his life. He became a systems engineer in 1996 and has spent years perfecting his trade, all the while building his pack of dogs at home. Through dog ownership and the challenges of living with a "pack" of dogs, he has studied dog behavior, finally landing him at Penn Foster College where he graduated as a dog obedience instructor. Both Kenneth and Cindy have worked with special-needs pets ranging from the timid, fearful, deaf, and hyper to those exhibiting human and dog aggression.

In training dogs with behavioral problems, Kenneth and Cindy quickly realized that owners unknowingly caused many of these problems. They also recognized the mistakes that puppy owners were making when it came to raising their new puppy. That and the fact that after years of working with clients and answering questions ranging from puppy start-up to temperament problems, Kenneth and Cindy developed the Puppy Montessori program and Super Mutts canine rehabilitation and training systems.

Kenneth and Cindy Quigley continue to own and operate Super Mutts. They reside in Arizona with their two dogs Rudy and Bentley. For more information, you can visit them at www.supermutts.com and www.facebook.com/supermutts.

Made in the USA
Middletown, DE
01 February 2022